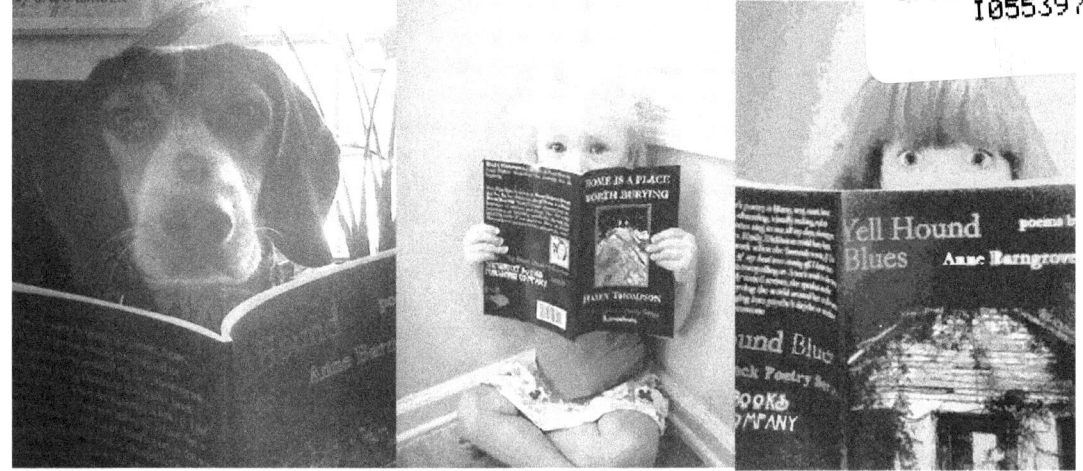

Discerning readers shop online at
www.shipwrecktbooks.com

Lost Lake Folk Opera

DEDICATED TO BELOVED NOTORIOUS RBG, JUSTICE RUTH BADER GINSBERG.

Covid-19 2020 Issue

Volume 6

Contents

SHIPWRECKT BOOKS PUBLISHING COMPANY L.L.C.

Rocket Science Press
Lost Lake Folk Art

Up On Big Rock Poetry Series
Lost Lake Folk Opera

Lost Lake Folk Opera is a Shipwreckt Books imprint
published annually.
Letters to the editor are always welcome.

309 W. Stevens Ave.	Rushford, Minnesota, 55971
507 458 8190	contact@shipwrecktbooks.com
Managing Editor	Tom Driscoll
Publisher	Beth Stanford

www.shipwrecktbooks.press

www.shipwrecktbooks.press

Cover art, interior graphics and photography by Shipwreckt Books.

"Victoria" by Roger McKnight was previously published in his short story collection, *Hopeful Monsters*, Storgy Books, 2019.

We acquire First North American Serial Rights (FNASR) upon acceptance and retain exclusive rights to your submission for six months following publication. Your piece will be archived and may be included in future retrospective editions. If you republish your work, please attribute first publication to *Lost Lake Folk Opera* magazine.

Covid-19 2020

www.shipwrecktbooks.press

Emilio DeGrazia
My Viral Summer Vacation

 o vacate means to empty out or go away, but I'm still at home with my Social Security check locked in for another few months, perhaps.

Minnesota winters have hardened me to viral life. In winter I circle and swirl, mainly in my head where thoughts rise like yeasty bread, half-baked. I'm also fortunate to suffer from imagination deficiency. Try conjuring the faces of thousands of virus victims. I can't. And my pigmy heart is too puny to make enough room for them. I'm also unscientific enough to conclude the virus is Nature's way of asking us all to try Business as Unusual. It's a tiny horrendous disease, with a grim sense of humor clever enough to leave in its wake cleaner city air, back to basics behaviors, inner resource development opportunities, and a widespread sense of mutual dependency.

As a retired college prof I brood about how the virus will infect public education systems already being undermined by billionaires who want to privatize them all. Most of all I'm troubled by Progress pandemics pushed by careless entrepreneurs. They're all for Growth, even as some growths swell out of control and turn poisonous. I tell everyone that Mary Shelley's *Frankenstein,* written when she was 18 years old in 1819, is the most important book of the 21st century. The monster in it, the brainstorm of a Ph.D. mind, was engineered by a privately enterprising doctor hooked on what he could achieve without seriously asking about where his project might lead him. (Mary Shelley's last novel, *The Last Man*, is about a disease.) The technologies we so brilliantly create keep morphing into monsters out of control, like those industrialized weeds that make Roundup gag. My car is useful and fun, but I try to banish all thoughts of the oil wars and pollution pandemics car grilles cheerfully bring to us. Now I see a digital pandemic coming my way, already at home in my home. My computer is smaller than my car, and it too has uses and fun potential. I type and print with it, and respond to hundreds of emails every week. I also try to be less unnatural. No cell phone owns me yet. I'm shaky and mouthy, but I don't twitter yet. I ache when I run, so I don't like to Zoom. I prefer to spend time with my nose, not my face, in a book. And now remote learning, its Progress smoothed by digital addiction of innocent young people with stooped necks, is becoming the "higher ed" rage. Learning is "distanced." No one says "less humanized."

I see silent liberal arts heads rolling off the chopping block, wide-eyed with backward gazes at college campuses that once upon a time were actual places where young people performed rites of passage with a few new good ideas turning in their minds. I recall smallish classrooms full of the energy of those ideas. I have dimming memories of honest hard-earned research, grounded in humane debate, contributing to a cumulative body of knowledge. Campus life—especially the liberal arts and humanities that have been its heart, soul and mind—is an endangered species now, slyly being eased out, privatized. I see science, civics, civility, critical thinking and knowledge losing institutional presence and authority, devolving into distracting ads and info-bits that disappear into a black hole internet dominated by business and entertainment profiteers, political operatives, and whackos. I see us rushing wildly into that black hole, unhappily.

Meanwhile, I feel very lucky. I'm a material beneficiary of all the terrible wars politicians and business leaders failed to prevent. In 1967 I ventured scared and alone across the Berlin Wall into East Germany, just to look around. One main impression remains: A grocery store with empty shelves, one solitary orange and one chocolate bar pathetically on display. I, however, have plenty of goodies on my pantry shelves. In stores I buy big bags of flour to keep my half-baked ideas rising well fed out of bed every day. I have a big house and a garden in my yard. I have three really nice children, a kind, smart, hard-working and lovely wife Monica. I have plenty of paper and pens, too many unread books, and wonderful neighbors and close friends. I enjoy vacation cruises in my mind without paying for gas and parking fees, and what I call work most people would call play. I don't have to hurt my back picking the beans I buy in stores, or slaughter the pigs, or cut them into tidy chunks. Nameless poorly paid migrants do most of that, and I'm socially distanced from them. I do miss long talky dinners with good friends. But I follow doctors' orders. I can't wash my hands of everything, but I wear my mask. Everyone says it improves my looks.

Larry Gavin

An Assemblage of Troubles: May 26, 2020

Outside the window,
Brick walls on three sides, and just a glimpse of blue sky.
In a honey locust a Kestrel appears occasionally all day,
fierce, as I wish I was fierce. But I'm not fierce.
I'm sick and weak.

Six blocks north, death in a gutter, George Floyd, murdered at the knee of cop.
Six blocks from my sickbed. There was nothing I could do. I could not beg the knee for mercy. "I can't breathe." He cried.
What has happened in this world devoid of grace? A world that has, for me at least, always been full of light at dawn, goldfinches, dogs and bright day.

The song has gone from the plowing. The melody of pines sung off key. Indeed, the music is sirens and heart break, not bird songs and hope. One question that
time will answer, if we are lucky, if not, it will answer anyway.

Julie A. Ryan
The Thoughts of a Polar Bear

I used to wonder what the polar bear was thinking when my children and I visited him at the zoo. I know that I had thoughts of rescuing him every time I watched him pace back and forth on his small patch of real estate, shaking his head from side to side in search of someone to play with. Or maybe his head was trying to do an Etch A Sketch-style erase of his understanding of the definition of insanity. After he lunged into his pool to do a few revolutions of a furry freestyle crawl, then climbed onto his piece of earth to resume pacing back and forth, I always fantasized about interrupting his routine. When I made eye contact with him, I'm sure he telepathically begged me to look for a hammer near his display window with a sign stating, "In Case of Emergency, Break Glass." I looked, but there wasn't one. So, all I could do was send my thoughts of freedom to the polar bear and hope that he felt encouraged.

Thoughts of that polar bear have become part of my pandemic routine that includes pacing back and forth in front of my dining room windows. Originally, I claimed that I paced on my small patch of real estate to collect enough Fitbit steps for my exercise goal each day. But after several months of retracing my path during my self-imposed isolation due to a compromised immune system, I've been forced to acknowledge that I'm doing it because I have nowhere else to go. I think this reality check was rudely tossed my way, like a dead fish, by my freedom-loving creative spirit that craves new experiences to digest.

My creative spirit is apparently unhappy with the pandemic cage I have placed myself in. For lack of new experiences to look forward to and process in prose, poetry, and paint, my expressions have become a reiteration of my history. Thoughts have been ricocheting off the same protective walls day after day, after day, and always land on a stack of memories from the past and questions for the future. Lately, my artwork has been very square-looking and my words have been boxy and stagnant when I try to portray this caged existence that has no release in sight.

I try to tell myself that simply existing right now is the most important thing and that participating in the arts has always been an act of unnecessary indulgence. The creativity isn't flowing in my penned up state, but I have a roof over my head, a place to safely rest at night, and I have access to an ample food supply provided by my zookeeper husband who goes out to do all my grocery shopping. Trivial matters like the number of Fitbit steps I accumulate and what shape my thighs are in have landed on the irrelevant pile concerning pandemic existence. So, these days I find myself pacing around my dining room table simply to help convince my creative mind that, as long as I'm moving, I am free.

I believe I now know what the caged polar bear thinks. Please send your thoughts of freedom my way. This is an emergency.

Louis Martinelli

The Day the Virus Came

The earth was dying
The coral reefs shrinking
The rain forests without trees
The stock market soaring
The rich cheering
The virus spread wherever
There were people
It swam into their lungs
It filled them up
Some could no longer breathe
The angel of death came for them
Others hid alone dying from fear
In cities covered by smog
The night sky cleared
Stars appeared after many years
Of being hidden
Experts gave daily briefings
Counting bodies
As in a war
In the park picnic tables
Were wrapped in orange plastic
To prevent contamination

Masked citizens wanting to live
Appeared in public resembling
The Lone Ranger
The President said not to worry
The virus will disappear
It will be a miracle
Women no longer invited
Men into their beds
A farmer helping
A cow give birth
Was kicked unconscious
And died in the hospital
The zoo closed where long ago
The last passenger pigeon died
Time stood still
The three Fates stopped weaving
The present from the future
When the virus goes away
The earth will be dying
The coral reefs shrinking
The rain forests without trees.

Emilio Regina

My Uncle and The Corona

y ninety-three-year-old uncle possesses two juxtaposing sides: one humorous, the other grave. At times I don't know when he's pulling my leg or when he's dead serious. Both qualities have their entertainment value, but what's unfortunate is when he becomes intense in either state, as his fervency robs his memory, ruthlessly and indefinitely.

I'm presently house sitting his place which suits me well. As my Uncle puts it, the house sitting is "temporary" because he plans on coming back to do some major renos with his trusty wooden-handled hammer. He's in an old folks' home, so I call to check up on him every other day. Last night he told me he was sipping on a Corona. He assured me not to worry about that brand of brew, that it was perfectly safe to drink. He figured there were no living viruses swimming in it, or they would have taken it off the market years ago.

"That's not what's killing us, Frank," he postulated like as if he had made some major discovery for the better of humankind. He went on and on about the coronavirus and the brew and I just listened intrigued by his nonsensical antics. He concluded it was not the Corona brew that was doing us in but something else. Then there came a pregnant pause in this one-way conversation. I missed my cue and should've asked the obvious.

"Are you with me, Frank?!" he exclaimed. I assured him I was. He was flaring up. Not a good sign. But he remembered my name, a certainty he hadn't tripped into some dark hole.

"So what's the real cause of this pandemic?" I ventured to ask my uncle. My uncle, who would sit us all down when our ages where but single digits and recite some of his poetry or read stories he had published. My Uncle, who would tell us how his ideas would evolve as he clunked away into the wee hours of the morning. Tap, tap, tap one letter at a time.

"Well it wasn't easy for me to figure out, Frankie boy." I could hear him at the other end triumphantly sipping his beer on the sly. The beer I would smuggle into the eldercare home. "Fact is Frank, it might be infecting you right now and you're totally oblivious to it. But you can trust your uncle on this one. It's all in the name."

"What's in a name?" I asked at the expense of sounding dumb.

"The name 'Coronavirus', obviously." This he stated with absolute conviction. It's as if the name were some secret code sent from the gods, something to crack. My Uncle went on to say, "The real solution is to get rid of what's causing it in the first place."

"So, what is this...this thing that's caused the pandemic?" I repeated.

"I was getting to that, Frankie, until you interrupted me."

"Sorry, Uncle."

"So you really want to know?" he asked with an air of pride and secrecy.

"Of course," I retorted with feigned sincerity.

"Ok, now we're getting somewhere. Where are you, Frankie?"

"I'm at your house, remember?"

"Of course I remember that. I thought you'd be on your cellphone somewhere else is all. And don't treat me like I'm losing my mind!" He was flaring up again. "Ok, so pay close attention," he demanded, "cause this thing is highly contagious. Put on a mask, grab one of those green garbage bags in the cupboard next to the fridge and I want you to go down to the root cellar cause that's where it is. No, no wait! Wait!! Are you waiting!!"

"Don't panic. I'm waiting." This I expressed with calm, knowing his ramped-up state could set him off and have his neural circuits collapse altogether.

"Ok, so grab three-THREE of those green garbage bags. You want to bag and re-bag it three times and send it off into space," my Uncle gravely instructed like he was going to save the world. It appeared he firmly believed in what he was saying. I played along.

"Are you still there? Frank?"

"I'm right here Uncle."

"Well stay focused! Never you mind about your date tonight!"

Who said anything about a date?

"Are you making your way down the stairs?"

"I'm a step ahead of you. I'm by the root cellar," I informed him.

"Now you don't want to open the door too quickly cause it'll cause a stir and then you'll catch it!"

"Catch what?"

"The virus! You nincompoop!"

"Ok, ok," I said getting wrapped up in his game.

"Now open the confounded door! Slooooowly!"

"Ok, it's opened. Ohhh!" I gasped for air.

"Frankie can you read me! Are you there!"

"Yes I can read you and I can smell the rank in here too. My god! Something crawled in here and died!"

"You'll be the next to die if you don't act quickly! Never mind the smell and get a hold of yourself! Focus, Frankie. Focus, FOCUS! FOCUS!!"

"Ok, Ok, Ok!" I shout into the phone.

"Now right beside the canned tomatoes on the middle shelf left hand side, I want you to lift the plastic covering. Do you see it?"

I saw it all right. I made the connection right then and there when I lifted the plastic covering. I couldn't help but chuckle into the phone. It wasn't the Corona beer but a Corona nevertheless. In all its classic splendor there lay, Uncle's old Smith Corona typewriter with the letters "h" and "a" depressed. I let out another chuckle. Oops.

"What in the Sam hell are you laughing at! Bag the damn thing! Bag it will you. BAG IT! BAG IT!! He yelped hysterically.

"Ok, Ok! Unc, take it easy," I sputtered trying to quell him. I could already tell I was going to lose him. "Unc, are you there?"

"Who is this?" he questioned with a voice from some other sphere.

"It's your nephew, Frank remember?" I knew too well where this was going.

"Who did you say?"

"Frank, Frankie."

"I don't know a Frank or a Frankie. You must have the wrong number." And just like that, click.

I'm sure he'll never leave the old folks' home, but some magic dust sprinkled my surety on the matter, and I think, who knows maybe one day he will come back and do major renos on his home with his wooden handled hammer in hand.

Jennifer Wang
जल्द ही

Jaldhee

I was thirteen when I first met you
In the smoking chaos that was Mumbai,
Your elbows hung over the steel railing looking out on the alley
Another cousin had come running,
Using the language of gesture:
Come
So I obeyed, turning nooks and crannies,
Until I peeked out the door
And suddenly it was just the two of us. And just as suddenly, I realized that had been
the plan all along.

At the time, I could only speak English, and fortunately you did too
Though haltingly
But your will was strong, your eagerness stronger
And I could see in your eyes the desire to know me
This foreign legend from the fair-skinned world.

We exchanged no more than a handful of phrases that afternoon
Until we were called in to lunch
And I gratefully retreated into the breeze of ceiling fans,
For here air conditioning was only for the rich,
And instead of struggling to form words to each other,
Our mouths were now occupied with the task of consuming
Spicy, sour, even tangy   Soaring
Flavors that made language unnecessary

Back inside, you were a different person.
No longer hesitant or bashful,
You carried out plate after steaming plate
That you helped your mother prepare.
Then cleaned up after all the mouths were closed and satisfied,
Restoring the mountain of crockery to their unstained state with that
Unyielding Smile,
Sleeves rolled up and curlicues damp from sweat and sudsy water.
Here there were no dishwashers nor vacuums,
Not even running water
But no matter—you were a Queen,

As you squatted to wipe the floor with bare hands
Making it seem as easy as reclining on the porch with a good book.

Fourteen years would pass before I saw you again
This time with a little bit of white to the right of my forehead
You brushed the tufts with concern,
Why?
Because I'm getting old, I joked. You laughed.
You were ten years older than me—thirty-seven without a single strand of
gray,
The dark pigments in your hair and skin impenetrably beautiful,

But now you were followed by shadows,
Nine and seven-year-old daughters.
They scurried in the folds of your *dupatta* scarf,
Hiding in your presence.
But as soon as you stepped away, called to this or that by your mother
They revealed themselves, chattering like red-crested bulbuls,
Asking me questions, consulting with each other on the proper English
translation
Even though I knew what they intended to find out
Before they uttered a word.

This trip was three months
And I had come alone
So the conversation on the veranda continued,
Stretching from minutes to hours
On the hard uneven planks of park benches,
Or walking side by side with linked arms,
Until midnight released the air's smoldering heat:
the shadows leaning from left to right
Front and Back
Pretending not to listen.

I was beaten, you announced
As casually as you shake salt into your *keema*.
Often? I asked, just as casually.
Only when I did something wrong, you replied.
You told me the older one loves her father dearly.
She cried every day when He was in jail for three months.
Her tomboyish dimple vanished.
But you only wept on the day of His release,
When you saw His fingers feathery from lice,
Tears wetting His now thinning scalp,

As you tweezered out the rest from His hair.

I didn't ask what He had done.
But you told me anyway:
He stole a car.
It was for us, you explained.
My doll head bobbed,
Like I understood.

You tried to explain.
He was the treasured first son of the family next door
On track to get a PhD and government job.
Until against their wishes,
He married you.
And just as they predicted,
He became a failed academic,
Trying to support a family
Who no one would hire.
And then there were the complications of gambling and drinking
Which you left out,
But secrets could not be kept in such close quarters
Emerging like dust settles on a window sill,
Inevitable over time.

By then Grandma—our King—made an edict:
Leave Him or leave her home.
Bringing up my father and your mother
And a tassel of other children without the help of fathers
She had only one rule.
Keep a man around only if he helped pay the bills.

Which He hadn't been doing
Even before He was taken away in handcuffs
And your landlord kicked you out,
Leaving you on Grandma's stoop Whose rage was only surpassed
By the softness of her heart.

Which she passed on to you.
You could not leave Him.
So you went to sleep on the hard uneven planks of park benches
Followed by your shadows
Who refused to let you go alone.
The three of you able to drift off anywhere
In the crooks of each other's arms,

Even on the bare earthen floor beside my steel bed,
its cold pillars proclaiming my American status,
That Unyielding Smile lasting the entire night
Playing on your lips like that of a blue-skinned god's.

You returned to Grandma's by day to sneak visits
Caring for me like a third daughter
With your magical talents,
The bite of mustard seeds,
Lingering—
My clothes hanging on your lines
After you had wrung and beat them against the flat rocks of the stoop.

On the first day of my internship,
Grandma—who'd forgiven you by then—insisted you accompany me,
But you had never taken the train
And though you led me by the hand
It was I who had to comfort you.
Even as ladies hit each other over the heads with purses in their rush to board,
It would all be fine.
We could just catch the next train.

But more than likely, we'd make this one—
Squeezed into gaps between fleshy armpits
Left bare by *cholis* a few sizes too small.
The metal poles just out of reach
So we stood clutching each other,
Held up by the sheer mass of the crowds,
Swaying as the train roared down the track
Decimating all that dared stand before it.

And then came that last day
Too quickly
The taxi Grandma hailed waiting out by the main road
Wet trails desecrating your smooth cheeks,
Rich as the cacao bean,
Until I wiped them away.
Holding back what brimmed in my chest
Because that's what I was used to.
But it wasn't just sorrow
For what I could never tell you
Was that by now I longed to be home.
To be in the arms of my He who was waiting.

My last image of you is standing by the roadside
Shouting,
Jaldhee
One hand outstretched,
Jaldhee
Your shadows echoing,
Jaldhee
In high-pitched unison,
Jaldhee
The other hand still clutching my plaid pajama bottoms.
I had offered them to you in case they would be useful
And you hid your real opinion behind that
Unyielding Smile
Nodding and Saying, Yes, to remember you by.

Jaldhee

Quickly, hurry, soon
You had taught me this word
Among so many others
Until I left the land of our ancestors
Able to speak their language,
Haltingly,
But good enough.

Jaldhee

You had urged me, both my hands in yours
Looking into my eyes
Making me promise

Jaldhee

Come back soon
Because in increments of fourteen years
We would only see each other two or three times more
If we were both lucky.

And you knew more than I in that moment
The pulls of life
So much more in my world
Erasing memory
With a tidal force.

So that already ten years had passed
When my father returned from a trip
And I asked about you.
He replied
As casually as you shake salt into your keema,
Your husband was dead.
Had been found years ago
Floating upside down in the river
That snaked murky through the slums.

Jaldhee

It triggered a memory from the abyss of my mind,
That the stolen car was supposed to repay a debt
to people who carried out their own justice.
But He had been caught…
You had wrung your hands, your smooth brow furrowed.
Until I told you not to worry.
People didn't commit murder for such a silly reason
Or get away with it.
In my world.

Jaldhee

But they did.
For days I thought of you
And worried
That Unyielding Smile
Evaporated
And what of the shadows?
Fatherless
For another generation.

Jaldhee

I felt like boarding a plane
But by then, my own shadows
Were cast,
A stormy web of intoxicating joy,
Whose needs bowled me over in torrential waves.
There was no way to extract myself
No way to bring them
And then I realized,

It was too late anyway.
You would have mourned long ago
Probably no longer even remembered
The touch of a man,
A reason for breasts other than for suckling.

Jaldhee

And now?
Sixteen years have passed since you waved at me by the roadside
We are almost going to be old women.
You sooner than me, I would joke.
But you are the one with white hair, you would laugh.

And yet the voices are only in my head.
Like that night I can still remember
In the cool of midnight
On the hard uneven planks of park benches
You turned to me
With the light of the moon glancing off black flint
And said,
A woman
Dreams too.

Jaldhee

Now I know for one of us those dreams never came true.
But what of the dream I can offer?
How many times I sit here in the sun
In the momentary bliss of three to four minutes
Of nothing to do
For once, emails sent off, dog fed, lunches made;
The shadows wreaking their havoc at school,
And think of reaching out my hand
To you
That Unyielding Smile
Brought back Just for a moment
I can dream too.
Jaldhee, Sister, it will be soon.

Becky Boling

Cabin 9

"It's not only here; it's everywhere.... Something has happened to the birds." Daphne du Maurier, "The Birds"

usan spit into the sink and watched the saliva ooze down the drain. The bitter tang of bug spray numbed the tip of her tongue. "Yuck," she said, though there was no one in the cabin to hear. Early that morning, Ralph had headed out, tackle box and pole, dressed in LL Bean vintage angler attire, ordered specifically for their trip to Bear Lake, just outside the boundary waters of northern Minnesota. Susan had tossed and turned on the damp, hot sheets, searching for a cool spot. The midsummer pollen had set off a thunderstorm of a headache that woke her at four o'clock in the morning. Taking his night crawlers and fishing rod, Ralph had left her to get another hour of sleep before she dragged herself from the bed to stand in front of the one-cup coffee maker, desperate for a bit of caffeine to ease her sinus headache.

She had recovered more or less after a third cup and an hour of sitting and admiring the view from the panoramic window that faced the lake. Between birch trees, a patch of sky leaned over the reflective surface of the lake. Headache aside, the moment was perfect. This was what it was all about, wasn't it? The picture-perfect scene was all the more remarkable cast within the precise limits of the window's cedar frame. Nature in all its beauty—packaged and presented for her enjoyment in a setting with all, or most, of the conveniences of home. It was easy to shake off the disappointments of their arrival the day before, now that the minor hurdles of shopping and settling in had been cleared.

She rinsed her cup in cold water with none of the concern that she usually had for cleanliness or germs. "There," she said as she set it to dry in the Rubbermaid drainer. She wiped her hands and checked her watch which never left her wrist. It was nearly eleven. He should have been back by now.

The buzz at her left ear reminded her of old movies with motorcycles spinning on gravel or small prop planes crossing the Atlantic. She jerked away and batted with open palms the air around her. A heavy black glob crossed her field of vision. The horsefly turned in a wide arc and then dove for her with instinctual precision. Eyes wide, she followed the trajectory as her hand groped for the flyswatter dangling strategically on a hook near the sink.

BZZZZZZ. Swat! Success!

Susan stared at the black fly, one wing quivering, on the kitchen counter. With satisfaction, she took a slip of paper towel and scooped it up. She dropped the dead insect into the waste bin and consciously relaxed her face muscles which had scrunched into an automatic display of disgust.

When they arrived last night, Ralph had surveyed the rooms for her, sweeping away any obvious signs of daddy long legs, spiders, beetles, or moths. He teased her mercilessly about her private war against bugs, but he hadn't grown up in the south where a medium-sized cockroach could carry off a slice of bread.

She looked again at her watch. Half past eleven, nearly lunch time. Where had the morning gone, and where was Ralph?

Her husband was a sometimes fisherman. He got the urge each spring, dusted off his tackle box, grabbed his fishing pole, went to the local bait shop, and discussed lures with townies who knew much more than he did about fishing, the outdoors, and Minnesota lakes and rivers. Who was he kidding? He grew up in Chicago, swam in heated pools, thought Lake Michigan was for tourists. The closest to nature he got was in his childhood when his parents sent him to Wisconsin for camp one week in the summer.

She decided to go down to the dock to see if she could catch a glimpse of the canoe Ralph had rented. She cast off her slippers and picked up her shoes. She batted the soles together hard. She had heard stories of spiders and other creepy-crawlies stowing away in innocuous-looking places like shoes.

Outside the cool air was already heating up in spots where the sun penetrated the canopy of birch, oak, and evergreen. Close to the water's edge, a thin line of deciduous trees testified to a fire that had raged through the wilderness area a few years ago. The tourist trade was just beginning to rebound. Susan and Ralph had perhaps lucked onto the last, best vacation deal for the foreseeable future.

She gingerly made her way across the clearing at the back of the cabin toward the floating dock. At the only cabin within hailing distance, a family of six seemed to be packing their SUV. Susan heard the doors clumping open and closed several times. One of the children was having a tantrum. A harried adult barked instructions, but Susan couldn't make out what the parent was saying. At mid-week, the family was already leaving?

Ralph had chosen Cabin 9 because it was the farthest from the lodge and the most private at the small camp. He liked the illusion of being self-sufficient and alone, as if the lake belonged only to them. In spite of the 4th of July holiday, only a handful of the cabins had been rented according to the web site where Ralph made the reservations. They had picked up the keys to the cabin and instructions at the agency in town that handled the rentals and had gotten to the camp by late afternoon. After unpacking the car, the sun was close to setting. Ralph and Susan had made their way down to the lake to take a quick swim.

Curiously, no one else was in the water. The closest docks had all been bare.

As Susan followed the path down to the lake, the rocky soil dug into the thin soles of her water shoes. She kept an eye out for local fauna, but her noisy approach was likely to scare off anything that might cross her path. The dock swayed sharply underfoot when she stepped out over the water. Ralph had warned her to be careful. She wasn't the most graceful person in the world. Arms out for balance, she reached the end and scanned the lake.

There were several islands in Bear Lake, and Ralph might be on the far side of any one of them, for he was nowhere in sight. A large bird, perhaps an eagle, soared overhead. She was watching, her hand shielding her eyes against the sun's glare, when something dull thudded against the dock, causing it to rock beneath her. She grabbed hold of a metal pole that jutted three feet from the water to the side of the dock. Her heart boomed in her chest, and she stared down into rust-colored water. Then she searched the surface for a sign of what had careened against the dock but saw nothing, just the rippling wake of something large.

*

Back at the cabin, Susan put out lunch. It was nearly one o'clock now. Ralph would be burned to a crisp. She was sure that he'd not have thought to put on anything but bug repellant. Ralph thought himself impervious to the sun.

She nibbled at her sandwich, waving her hand over the one she made for Ralph just in case a gnat or fly might take advantage. A few minutes later, she wrapped the sandwich and put it in the fridge, cleared the table, and cleaned the plates. She put on her sneakers, sprayed herself with insecticide, and headed for the camp office.

Cabin 8 was quiet, but curiously the SUV was still parked in the clearing next to the side door. She walked on and veered off into the woods, taking the shortcut to avoid the other cabins along the shoreline. She kept her eyes a few feet ahead, watching her step as she went.

A snapping sound, like the sharp crackle of burning wood, made her stop and look around. She waited, thinking perhaps she might catch a glimpse of a deer. Seeing only rows of trees, fallen limbs, and rotted tree trunks, she set off again, following the trail as it angled away from the lake.

Then, just ahead, a large, furry animal, a raccoon, lumbered directly into her path. She drew up sharply and stood still. So did the raccoon. The animal's whiskers twitched. Its snout pointed in her direction and sniffed at the air.

Susan's hands clutched at the fabric of her T-shirt, and she held her breath. She had never been this close to a wild animal before. The raccoon was much larger than she expected from images she'd seen on TV and in nature magazines: as big as a medium-sized dog. It blocked her path, seemingly in no rush to leave. There was nothing cuddly about it. At this distance, she could see the details of the black markings that gave it its bandit reputation, but what struck her were the paws. The raccoon lifted a paw, crooking and waving the long, individuated fingers as if it were beckoning for her to come nearer.

"Go away," she whispered, almost afraid of her own voice.

Instead, the raccoon rose on its haunches, bringing its head just below the level of her waist. Susan took a step backwards. The raccoon stretched its snout like a weapon and chittered loudly at her, making a clicking sound with its tongue and teeth. At the same moment, the forest burst into sound. The whirring of cicada joined the blasting croaks of what seemed to be hundreds of frogs, and the cawing of birds filled the sky overhead. The noise engulfed her, its volume ascending almost to the point of pain. She cupped her hands over her ears. Movement just beyond her peripheral vision evaded her each time she twisted to catch it.

She jerked her head back to look at the raccoon. It wasn't where it had once been. It had moved. Now mere inches away, it fixed its black bottomless pupils on her. She could see the pink inside of its maw as it opened its mouth wide.

Susan turned and ran clumsily over the roughened path. Something swooped past her, making her stumble and fall to her knees. Her palms burned as they scraped against the rocky soil. An army of black beetles spilled onto the path. A bulbous hornet flew at her mouth, hit just to the side of her lip, and bounced to the ground. She struggled to her feet. Swatting at a cloud of insects buzzing around her nose and eyes, she took off at a dead run.

Seconds later, she broke into the heavy sunlight. She slowed and glanced back over her shoulder. Breathing hard, she could hear nothing but the coursing of her own blood, the work of her lungs. The path behind her was empty. The forest had gone quiet. Nothing, nothing at all, not even the breeze made a rustle in the upper leaves of the trees.

Slowly, reluctantly, she forced herself to turn away from the woods. She needed to get back to the cabin. Later, she'd send Ralph to the camp office at the lodge. They had the only reliable phone service in the area. From the office, Ralph could get word to the manager who lived only ten minutes from the camp. He would explain about the raccoon. Perhaps it was rabid. Maybe the manager knew who to call so that someone would come and deal with the animal.

*

When she came within sight of the cabin, she saw that the door stood wide open. Ralph must have returned! She rushed inside, calling out for him. But no one answered. She called out again. Then she noticed the trail of wet grit on the floor. She followed it to the empty bedroom where it ended abruptly, just over the threshold. Annoyed, she sidestepped the gritty mess and followed it back to the living room. It led to the door that opened onto the raised deck. She peered out the large picture window onto the clearing and the lake beyond. There was no sign of Ralph.

Had he forgotten something in the canoe and gone back down to the lake? Susan went out onto the deck and down the stairs to the small clearing. The scrim of trees to the west blocked her view of cabin 8. She listened for any sound of her neighbors, but it was too quiet. No crying children, no angry adults. Had they already gone?

Quickly, she crossed the clearing and made her way down the steep bank to the dock. Halfway there, she saw the canoe but no sign of Ralph. Stranger still, the canoe floated a couple of feet from the dock. Its mooring line hung from the bow, disappearing into the water.

"Ralph!" she called at the top of her lungs, her hands cupping her mouth. Uneasily, she stepped out onto the dock and walked to the far end. The canoe was beyond the reach of her hand. Holding the metal pole, she stretched her left foot and tried to snag the rim to drag it to the dock. Just as she was about to catch the edge, she saw movement in the bottom of the canoe and jerked her foot back to the safety of the dock. Leaning over, she peered into the canoe.

Several fish lay in a shallow pool of water, gills gulping, eyes wide with rage, fins flapping. As she stretched to get a better look, a fish broke the surface of the lake on the far side of the canoe. Somersaulting into the air, it sprayed Susan, as far away as she was, with water. It landed with a heavy thud on the floor of the canoe, taking its place among the others.

Around the dock the water began to boil. Dozens and dozens of black fins cut the surface. Fish pummeled the dock with their bodies, making hollow noises. Out of the blue, one flew, like a projectile, from the water. It smacked Susan's upper arm and then rebounded to the wooden slats of the dock. Frantically, it jerked and beat the planks until it slipped back into the lake. Susan scrambled over the boards toward shore. But the dock swayed underfoot, and nearly within reach of land, she lost her balance. Her leg slid off the side of the dock, scraping her inner calf along the rough edge of the wooden plank and shearing a strip of skin from the ankle to just below the knee. Her foot hit the rocky bottom inches from the shore's edge. Her blood mixed with the water. A dark thing in the shallows swam forward, belly skimming on slippery stones. Susan yanked her foot from the water to the surface of the dock. She jumped the remaining distance between her and the bank and climbed the rustic steps, taking them so fast that she felt the jarring impact deep in the joints of her knees, ankles, and hips. She didn't slow down until she reached the clearing just outside the cabin. As she paused to catch her breath, something swooped overhead. A sharp pain seared a path across her scalp. She cringed and raised her hands and arms to fend off another attack, but the clawed creature rose over the clearing and flew to the upper deck of the cabin.

Birds! Perched in rows as precise as those of soldiers on parade, they covered every available, bare surface of the raised deck. Hundreds of them of all shapes and sizes, a hungry grasping mass of feathers and claws. The flapping of wings drew her attention away from the railing and deck chairs to the trees that overhung the clearing where she now stood transfixed.

Bowed under garlands of birds, the limbs of birch, oak, and beech rocked, swayed, sank, rose, and sank again. Visions of Hitchcock. Black birds on a jungle gym. Tippi Hedron trapped in the attic, batting at sparrows' wings. Susan crept forward, avoiding the besieged deck altogether, and headed for the screen door at the top of a short stoop.

Four steps were all that it would take and she'd be safe inside. She grabbed the handrail but jerked her hand away when she felt the wasp bury its stinger into the soft tissue between index finger and thumb. The venom's heat spread to the other fingers and across her palm. She swallowed a gasp and clambered up the remaining steps. Inside the porch, she yanked the door shut behind her. The susurration of insects drew her attention to the large rectangular screens that groaned, stretched, and bulged inward as swarms flew against the windows, wedging their abdomens and burying their stingers in the thin metallic mesh. Susan fled inside the cabin. Nearly falling into the living room, she managed to slam the interior door behind her, shutting off the screened-in porch.

She grabbed the keys from amidst a pile of clutter on the kitchen table and ran to the cabin's front door.

There was the car, just a few feet away, parked next to a fortress of trees. So close!

Here, too, they waited, winged and four-legged creatures, keeping vigil, alert, blocking her escape.

She dropped the keys on the floor and stumbled across to the opposite side of the room. There, she collapsed on the couch and faced the large picture window that overlooked the deck, the grounds below, and the lake beyond. But all she could focus on were the armies of sharp-beaked, winged creatures that stared back at her.

*

Within the next few hours, they came. They came from the water and the woods and the sky. More and more surged into the clearing, taking up positions, predator next to prey, all their attention directed upward toward the large picture window behind which Susan stared down at them. A menagerie gone wild occupied every inch of the clearing. Deer stood alongside wolves and raccoons. Squirrels, chipmunks, and small mammals that Susan didn't even have a name for occupied the space, sitting on top of the picnic table in the shade of a small oak tree, huddled around the outside pit where Ralph had built a bonfire to mark their first night at the cabin.

Ralph had been so proud when the sticks and dry leaves finally caught and burst into flames in the pit. He insisted on setting up two lawn chairs within the bright circle of its flames. They opened a bottle of wine and sipped from plastic cups. They had even made s'mores and roasted marshmallows over the fire, delighted that they were miles away from anything connected to their normal humdrum lives. Susan had tired quickly of the smoke buffeted willy-nilly by a contrary wind. It made her eyes burn and water, but Ralph said they should stay until there was nothing left but embers.

The next fire I make, he said, I'll find drier wood and I won't have to use so much lighter fluid. He went on to talk about the walleye he'd catch the next day and how they'd rig a way to cook the fish over the open pit, how much better it would taste than the fish they ordered at their favorite restaurant back home. Susan smiled and nodded, secretly dreading scraping the scales, dealing with fish guts and fine bones that could lodge in your throat and choke you. She didn't really believe that her husband would catch anything they could cook, but she didn't want to spoil his confidence and enthusiasm.

But Ralph wouldn't build that fire, would he? He was not coming home.

She stepped away from the window. They were out there. Nothing could shield her. Between her and them, there lay only the thickness of wood and glass.

*

Hours later, the sun sank slowly, so slowly that Susan identified the varying palette of colors in the only narrow patch of sky visible to her over the water until the last rays were extinguished. She sat wrapped in a blanket despite of the sultry heat. She waited in the dark now. She couldn't bear to light the candles or turn on a lamp because it would make it impossible for her to see through the glass panes the animals that were still out there, surrounding the cabin.

She sat with the cell phone in her lap, staring at the screen, watching the spinning lights as it searched for a signal. They had chosen this, being "off the grid," hadn't they? Ralph had left his iPad, and she had agreed not to bring her laptop. How pleased they had been that there was no television, no cable, not even a radio at the camp. After several more seconds, still no bars showed in the upper corner of the screen. Then, the same message she had seen over and over again appeared. "No service."

Where was Ralph? Had they attacked him while he was fishing that morning? Was he floating face down somewhere in the lake? She wept, making as little noise as possible, wanting to be as small and invisible as she could manage. But what about the wet, gritty streaks on the floor when she had come in? What had made them? Where had it gone?

Mosquitoes droned about her eyes, mouth, and ears. She had long ago run out of bug spray. Ignoring the flying insects, she gripped a flyswatter tightly in her right hand and kept her eyes pinned on the upper corner of the window. A large spider dangled from the frame, spinning an ever-expanding web.

*

The squeal of the screen door on the porch startled her. Her cell phone, the battery long dead, clattered to the floor. She threw off the blanket and stood.

"Ralph? Is that you?" she cried out.

Somewhere outside, the door to the porch snapped back in place. She heard heavy footsteps, the sound growing louder as they approached.

Relief flooded over her. Still holding the flyswatter, she made her way in the dark to the door between her and the porch. As she was about to reach out, the knob jiggled. But it did not turn. It was as if he had forgotten how to open it.

She called out again, her voice more uncertain this time. There was no response.

Fear told her to bar the door. But before she could grab the handle to hold the door shut, it swung open. The moonlight was barely enough to make out the thick outline of a man.

She recognized him immediately.

"My God, I thought you were dead!" she said.

His features were obscured by the darkness, but she knew him from his height and build, the way his left shoulder sagged a bit lower than his right.

She dropped the flyswatter and stepped back toward the table to search for the flashlight. She picked it up and turned it on him, careful not to shine the beam into his eyes.

The shaft of light fell across his feet. One of his shoes was missing. Water dripped onto the floor and pooled around the bare foot that she stared at with growing disquiet. She made out streaks of green slime and mud on pale flesh. She guided the unsteady light up the legs of his jeans to his waist and torso. She recognized his favorite blue and white checkered shirt. The fabric was drenched in lake water and stained by sediment. Her limbs began to shake. She had to clutch the flashlight with both hands to keep from dropping it.

In a weak voice, she whispered her husband's name.

Fishing line encircled his chest, wrapping around him several times, pinning his upper arms to his sides. She raised the angle of the flashlight higher to shine on his throat and chin. Then the edge of the light reached his slack mouth. The curve of a metal fishhook protruded from his bloodless upper lip, pulling the corner of his mouth up and to the side in a grotesque grin. The narrow beam of light fell on dulled, milky white eyes, rimmed with lake water. Something crawled from his left nostril and disappeared between his lips.

Her grip on the flashlight loosened. It clattered to the floor, extinguishing the light. Behind her husband, hundreds of feral eyes gleamed.

Ralph stepped inside the room.

Steve McCown

Two Pandemic Poems

Singing in a Pandemic

For Barbara Belobaba

Behind closed doors
the elderly listen.
Some move lips,
some toe-tap,
some harmonize.

"You are my sunshine,
my only sunshine.
You make me happy …"

A masked Piaf
wandering the hallways
of a Care Center,
she sings to the vulnerable,
the little sparrow
of her voice winging
into quarantined rooms,
alighting on ears,
ruffling silence.

"Welcome to my world.
Won't you come on in?

Miracles, it seems, happen now and then …"

But if they open doors
and wheel out to sing with her,
or if they hold hands
in a circle, the songs
will fall flat,
every last lyric,
every last word,
airborne.

"… I'll fly away.
Like a bird from these prison walls has flown,
I'll fly away."

How to Handle Personal Mail in a Pandemic

Don't touch the stamp.
Someone licked it.
Shun the back flap.
A tongue sealed it.

Undoubtedly, Covid lungs
hacked on your inked name.
If there's a return address,

don't thank the sender.
It might encourage her or him.

Knife slit it,
shake contents out,
dump them like junk mail,
or trash the missives whole
without the gutting.

If you must write,
write to yourself.
Use post-its and
plaster your walls
with fragments,
notes on yellow paper,
short lists, song lyrics,
grocery items
you shouldn't buy.

Replace the scrawls weekly.

Reading words
other than your own
is dangerous.
If the world keeps
writing to you,
move to a desert
ghost town where
only the Pony Express
might reach you,
or inhabit an abandoned
Inca city in the clouds.

Tell no one.
Leave no forwarding address.
Stick to yourself
like a fading post mark

Jim Johnson
Hooks

 f civilization should, and it looks like it most likely will, go the way, the way of Huehuetenango, then I, if I and any others do survive, will miss a few things. Fine leaders, not political leaders, but monofilament or fluorocarbon leaders. And, of course, hooks. I think I, together with my fellow leftovers from the hood once known as civilization, could make up the rest. I think I could fashion some kind of rod from bamboo-like strips with a line, probably made from gut, attached Tenkara-style. I know I could tie flies from spare animal fur and remaining bird hackles. But they would need to be tied to a hook. Maybe we could introduce a very small iron age. The Just-For-Hooks Iron Age. Maybe make a few knife blades too.

Hooks are important to a Not-Even-Close-To-Apocalypse Civilization, the kind I envision with cooperation and trade--trading for hooks, fine-line blacksmith hooks on which to tie flies with the thread we spin and survival species hackles. We will trade for food. Or for trout, so the trout must stay. Can you imagine a world without trout? Insert Trout Unlimited add here. Could you even live in a world without trout? Maybe it is time for proactivity. Just as the Guatemalan poet Otto Rene Castillo has told us no apolitical intellectuals will survive the revolution, no apolitical anglers will ever wade across and gather on that other shore. No sir.

Now let me get to the point.

The hook is what is between the fisherman and the trout, between predator and prey, between fish and human. Without the hook the fisherman would rather be a trout. At this point—drums drumming, bells shaking, and mantra after mantra—reincarnation becomes a feeder to the stream of consciousness. While the devil is nothing but a spear fisherman. But we anglers, we trout fishermen, we few fly fishermen stand up with a conscience.

And hooks.

Once while fishing the headwaters of Iowa, I hooked a rainbow trout that hooked me to my own fly. I had tied on a size 20 Partridge and Olive, to the bend of which I added a length of 5X tippet, then knotted a size 18 Bead Head Pheasant Tail onto the other end. The top fly drifted down and across near the surface while the slightly heavier bead head tied to the dropper sank, but at the end of the drift rose up and away from the trout, and the trout, as we all would, struck, struck out at what was getting away. That was the theory, but this rainbow had taken the Partridge and Olive top fly. After I had unhooked it, or thought I had unhooked it, and released, the rainbow flashed toward the quick and easy water, about 18 inches, for that was the distance between the flies, the length of my dropper, and ow! Did I tell you it was a Tiemco 200R size 18? A Tiemco 200R size 18 now ripped into my left hand, into and through the callous pad below my little finger. With my left hand somewhat as my rod, I pulled the struggling yet-hooked rainbow back and with my right hand managed to free the fish from the Partridge and Olive, and the rainbow flashed back into the this-time living water.

But the hook, the Tiemco 200R size 18, did I tell you? was in my left hand.

With the thumb and forefinger of my right hand I tried to pull the hook back and out. As I pushed it back and forth, even the slightest, the tendon or ligament the hook had found sent a nerve cry through my entire hand. The barb was set. The hook hooked deep inside.

I'm hooked, I said to you.

And you, my love, were with me. I am so glad you are with me now. But on that day I was especially glad I wasn't alone.

You said, Just push it through.

Just push it through? Of course, you were right as love always is. And I tried but felt the tendon/ligament groan. The hook wouldn't push.

I can't, I said.

Yet I knew I had to push the hook through, far enough that I could cut off the barb.

I'll just push it through, I said to you.

A Tiemco 200R size 18 is a small hook (thin as a mouse whisker, smaller than a cricket leg, about the size of an ant's backbone, if an ant had a backbone) and this one was inside my left hand. Taking out my pliers, usually used for unhooking trout, I set the jaws to the protruding shank near the eye and pushed, pushed back again until a sliver of hook, the point, penetrated my skin just as blood seeped around it, and then pushed yet again until the point pointed out of the blood and I felt the barb catch outside the surface of my skin.

Next I needed to carefully cut off the hook just below the barb, but there were no cutters on my pliers! Why didn't I have cutters on my pliers? It was wrong not to, so wrong, and so wrong too to have never checked.

Could I bend the hook back and forth until the shank broke off? The instant I began to bend sent the answer along the nerve through the tendon/ligament. The answer, in the plain language of pain, was No!

So there I was—my hand hooked to a Bead Head Pheasant Tail Soft Hackle, tied to a tippet, tied to the top fly Partridge and Olive, tied to a leader, tied to a Rio fly line, spooled to a Hardy LRH reel, mounted on a Phil Johnson bamboo fly rod. I was hooked. My hand, like a leaf in the air, hooked.

Did I need to back the hook, barb and all, all the way, plowing back through tendon/ligament nerve screaming all the way back and out, did I?

Yes, I did. But then I realized I could now pinch down the barb with my cutterless pliers. O yes, I did. Then I set the jaws of the pliers to the bend of the hook and yanked and, in that lightning shaped instant, out came the hook, a spray of blood, and a flood of relief.

I remember you gave me a tissue to sop the blood and a hug too. I didn't want to let you go but wondered what was that itching, itching my forearm, as I was holding you so tightly now that I was unhooked. As I flexed my hand, the joint now free, and looked at yikes! nettles. I was sitting, hugging you, you hugging me, in nettles. Green nettles so wonderful, but yet asking the ever-expanding question, What next?

I certainly had to think about what that trout must have felt, not only to have been hooked and unhooked twice, but taken out of its living water. Do we know what we do to fish? Should we become merely fish watchers? Or should we catch what we need to eat, and in eating give proper ceremony to the trout we eat, but stop fishing once we have caught our dinner? Should I not practice, now that I've experienced it, catch and release? Should I unhook myself from guilt and ever fishing again? From guilt, yes. From fishing, no.

For fishing for trout is what takes me in, not only to the beautiful places where trout survive, but to the wild I would not otherwise experience. To fishing and eating the ceremonial trout I know I am forever hooked.

The rainbow was released and lived again. I too was hooked and released, though I was forced to pause. But I know it is time, amid the pause before apocalypse, to push down my barbs and at least go barbless.

Waliyullah Tunde Abimbola
The Suicide Episode

At a café in a University. Jingo and Bongo are sitting opposite each other.

Bongo

See, I am tired of this school. How can I do seven courses in a semester and have no A? I don't think I can withstand this anymore. And if I tell my parents that I am not interested in school anymore, they would ask me to go and learn a handiwork. Maybe Carpentry or Tailoring. And I don't want that too. In fact, I am tired of this life.

Jingo

So what do you want to do?

Bongo

I think I'll … I think I'll just end everything. I'll cross over to the great beyond to roam around in Paradise with Jesus Christ our Savior.

Jingo:

So you will kill yourself?

Bongo

I thought you are the smart one. Do I need to spell every word before you understand?

Jingo

Sorry. Look, if you are telling me this so I can try to stop you, you are mistaken. Far be it from me to stop a fellow from doing what his heart desires. (*Incredulous, Bongo stares at him.*) So when is it going to be?

Bongo

You are a wicked soul. You want to me to die so … wait. What will you gain from my death?

Jingo

Nothing significant. Only that the number of us competing for the girls in our class will reduce.

Bongo

I should have known. You have never been my friend. You're just a green grass under the green … eh … what is that final part?

Jingo

It is green snake under green grass. What I wanted to tell you before you called me a wicked soul was that even if you will relocate to Heaven, you should wait till July, after that SpongeBob SquarePants movie has been released.

Bongo (*Snaps his fingers.*)

Ha, yes! That's right. I totally forgot. If I died and they told me in Heaven that I missed the SpongeBob SquarePants movie, I would throw a tantrum there.

Jingo:

With who? The Archangels? They would beat your stupid ass up. That aside. How are we even sure you are going to Heaven? You could end up in Hell.

Bongo (*Frowns.*)

What are you saying? Why would I not go to Heaven? I don't drink, I don't smoke, I don't steal and I go to church regularly.

Jingo

But you cheat in exams, you lie to your parents so they could pay you double of how much you actually need and you watch porn.

Bongo

All those are minor sins. They can't stop me from entering Heaven. You don't know the difference between major and minor sins since you don't go to church. Well, that settles it. I'm not going to the great beyond anymore.

Jingo

No. Don't let that deter you. You can always go after you've watched the movie.

Bongo (*Looks at him depreciatingly.*)

Why don't you strangle me to death immediately the cast and crew of the movie starts scrolling on the screen? Idiot. We will see this programme out together. This programme called 'Life'.

Finis

A. S. Arcilesi

Plastic Breath

fter seven days of intolerable confinement, Izzy decided that this foggy afternoon was the right time to free herself. And, if she could manage, Clara.

She had been testing her crippled body since the morning darkness, inundating her extremities with signals to flex, and, with any hard-earned luck, *move*. Her weak arms appeared up to the task; she guessed her weight to be just shy of one-hundred pounds. Her legs, however, remained stubborn, anchoring her to the bed. For all the training she had subscribed to these counterparts, none was more rigorous, more vital than her breathing regimen.

Izzy's relationship with oxygen had always been of a toxic nature. A university athlete who had relied upon her immaculate lungs for victory, it had been an unreliable ankle that decided ten metres from an important finish line was the time to snap, end her career, sink her into the depths of depression, and enroll her in a new, lifelong sport: smoking. Three packs a day, four when she was feeling particularly good (or bad), for fifty years.

And now the ghosts of cigarettes past were preventing her, despite her cooperative arms, from liberating herself, and, more importantly, Clara.

Izzy exhaled a laboured breath, painfully inhaled another. She should have been accustomed to it by now, but the air filtering throughout her sanctuary still tasted as artificial as it smelled. She felt the rather stale intake race through her mouth and nostrils, hoping to reach the pair of black bags that kept her going for no real purpose.

Save for Clara.

The clean dose of oxygen reached her ashen lungs, then exited her mouth and nose in another laboured exhalation. Izzy imagined the polluted molecules warning the new wave of respiration about what corruption lay within her.

She looked to her right, locked eyes with the never-blinking Clara, and, with a look that said "Don't you dare move now"—she couldn't risk precious breaths on her roommate's deaf ears—began the arduous journey.

Izzy watched as she willed her right arm across the centimetres that felt like kilometres of bed. The feeble limb made pitiful progress before stopping entirely so she may regain what energy she could.

A surge of anger propelled her arm against the plastic sheet dividing her and Clara. Her hand slid down the thick material until it landed in the crevice between the sheet and edge of the bed. Using this newfound leverage, Izzy began pulling her weight with her right arm, while pushing against the mattress with her left. The juicy idea of giving up had crossed her mind, just as it had when her former severely fit self, besieged by physical and psychological cramps, had desired to slow her run to a crawl at the three-thousand-metre mark. Her conditioned lungs had burned then. Now they were volcanic.

But the agony and certain death would be worth it. Not only for herself, but Clara, who had never felt a pang in her endless life.

Izzy now found herself at a ninety-degree angle: the top half of her body sprawled laterally across the bed; the bottom half remained affixed to where it had been since she embarked upon this suicide mission of sorts. After a quick mental team huddle with her barely working parts, she used her right hand to push against the plastic sheet. The damn thing was like a wall of concrete. Her reluctant body threatened to pull the plug on the whole operation, but a little bit of that wholesome anger, and a lot of thinking about what would happen to Clara if she failed, helped free the bottom of the plastic sheet from between the mattresses. Izzy exhaled so deeply, the fog outside of her only window found its way to her eyes.

One breath.

Her vision slowly...

Two breaths.

...slowly...

Three breaths.

...returned.

She felt her old nemesis oxygen assisting her rushing blood to restore her vision. But she knew better; death had brushed past her.

Move it, she urged herself.

Izzy hadn't intended to escape by falling on her head, but as she shimmied herself closer...

closer... closer, then over... over... over the edge of the bed, it seemed the only way. Her head free of the plastic sheet, the faint aroma of cooking bombarded her olfactory. She couldn't help but sacrifice a valuable breath to take in the recipe she had shared with her daughter long ago. *You're using too much garlic powder*, she thought, the seasoning burning her sinuses. But that was Isabelle: too much or too little of everything.

Her shoulders hanging over the edge of the bed, thinned blood rushing to her head, Izzy wondered—not for the first time—what Isabelle would think when the time came to trudge upstairs, check on her dying mother, and find her however she ended up. *Hopefully, with Clara in my arms*, she thought.

She wondered if her daughter would even care.

The pair of Izzys had lived a life of few kisses and plenty of bites. Izzy had made the cliche attempts to live via her namesake (Isabelle's ankles were still intact, after all). Her daughter had indeed run; not on the track, but away from home, turning the typical one-off act of rebellion into a quarterly sport. When she *was* home, Isabelle would blame Izzy for all of her life's unwanted biographic details: the casting out of her father, the selfish act of naming her after herself (never mind the tradition), the reason for her isolating unattractiveness, the asthma and other varieties of respiratory ailments courtesy of her chain-smoking. That her only child had decided to punish her by never marrying, never having children, was not lost on Izzy. Still, when Izzy had become too ill to breathe on her own, it was Isabelle who rushed her to the hospital; and it was Isabelle who brought her home, tucked her into bed, and made sure the oxygen tent kept her alive.

But after seven days of intolerable confinement, seven days of embarrassing baths and changes, seven days of no words exchanged save for begrudged greetings and farewells, Izzy had decided that this foggy afternoon was the right time to free herself. And, if she could manage, Clara.

Beloved Clara.

She could no longer see her only friend, but knew she was right where she had left her. *I'm coming*, she thought, hoping the suffocating air out here wouldn't render her a liar.

Like in the old days, when slower competitors somehow cruised past her, good old-fashioned anger fuelled her cause, and she writhed her dangling body further over the edge of the bed like a fish out of water. *A fish that wants out of her damn bowl!* she goaded herself, and grew angrier at her handicap. The fingertips on her right hand touched something cold, hard. It took her a moment to realize she had touched the floor. Her left hand, still pushing against the bunched-up comforter, worked alone to send her over the rest of the way.

In the space of seconds, Izzy saw the ceiling, then her abdomen, then her legs, the latter two crashing down on her. Within the same seconds, she had felt emptiness beneath her, then the same cold, hard floor forcing itself into her neck and spine. Precious breaths were knocked out of her, and the fog returned, this time most certainly accompanied by death.

It took her a few moments to realize that death smelled an awful lot like garlic. A few more moments, and Izzy understood she hadn't died... and that her daughter wouldn't have heard a thing if she had. She remained alone. On the floor. Alive. For now.

Alive enough to save Clara.

Slowly, surely, Izzy wriggled away from the bed until her dumb legs hit the floor. Still, her daughter remained downstairs, oblivious, or willfully so. But in case obliviousness turned to awareness, Izzy needed to move as quickly as her lame body would allow at this late stage in the race. *Last one hundred metres*, she implored.

Since sitting herself up was impossible, she needed to figure out how to get Clara to come down to her level. *Could've just grabbed her, and brought her into the tent*, she scolded herself, *save yourself this stupidity*. But she knew it wouldn't have been fair to Clara, to have her lifelong companion go from breathing one brand of plastic air to another. No. She wanted Clara's first breath to be one hundred percent, certifiable oxygen... even if it was tinged with garlic.

Izzy flexed the fingers on her left hand, expecting to feel a break, akin to that long-ago ankle, which would prevent her from crossing *this* finish line. Everything felt in working order. Hand shaped like a spider, the fingers crawled along the floor until they found the nightstand's feet. They climbed past the bottom drawer, then the middle, then-

She stopped, having reached as high as she could go. She looked at the progress her hand had made and was angered and disappointed to see the tips of her fingers so close to the top. So close to Clara.

No longer able to uphold itself, her arm fell to the floor for her daughter not to hear. Her shallow, disparate breathing became shallower, more disparate. The retinal fog grew thicker. And she was certain the last time she would see Clara was in the memories she had very limited time to relive:

Sneaking into her late mother's bedroom—this very same bedroom—to sneak a peek at Clara, high on her shelf.

Receiving Clara on the eve of her mother's passing—in this very same bedroom—on the condition that she pass Clara on to *her* daughter, should she have one, when her own end was near.

Asking Isabelle to take Clara off the shelf and sit her on the nightstand; the plan to release Clara had been confirmed, all the more so by her daughter's routine sneer and remark: "Ugly thing."

Even had Isabelle loved Clara as much as she had, Izzy felt it *her* duty to finally free her.

Come on, you useless cigarette-holder. Last fifty metres.

Her nicotine-stained spider-hand rediscovered the nightstand's feet, and, once more, began its ascent.

Past the bottom drawer.

Forty metres.

Past the middle drawer.

Thirty metres.

Past the bottom of the top drawer.

Twenty metres.

Finding the top drawer's knob...

Ten metres.

...where it hung...

Come on.

...unwilling to move.

COME ON!

Her hand sprang back, the drawer with it.

Sliding.

Sliding. Sliding.

Until the heavy piece abruptly stopped, having reached its limit. The nightstand leaned slightly forward, and Izzy glimpsed her legacy as the dead meat filling of a floor-and-nightstand sandwich. But the nightstand had other plans; before it settled back into place, it made sure to shake free the tall, glossy box.

The impact was painful, a sharp corner hitting her perfectly in the eye, but nothing compared to the torture her lungs were putting her through. Instead of fog, there was rain. Izzy blinked the burning tears away, bringing not the nightstand into focus, but a face.

And what a beautiful face it was. Skin made of meringue. A faint smile on pink lips barely formed. Rosy cheeks forever pinched into dimples. Black eyebrows arching over a pair of unblinking bejeweled eyes. Had they seen Izzy? *All* the Izzy's?

From Grandma Izzy to this sorry-excuse-for-an Izzy?

They stared at each other for some time, Izzy refusing to blink, like her little friend, lest she slip into death during one of those slivers of blackness. The smell of garlic was fading. She couldn't tell if her daughter was altering the recipe in some way, or if her senses were gradually shutting down.

Last ten metres, she thought. Perhaps her final thought.

Izzy used the left hand that made this final reunion possible to locate the pristine cardboard flap above Clara's head. Not with anger, but love, Izzy tore open the lid that had sealed the doll in her prison for three generations and watched as Clara took in her first-ever breath of fresh air.

James Petrillo

Twice Feckless

Two Sentence Horror Story

The feckless coward fingers the enter key, launching radioactive projectiles to rain death on billions. "Fake news," he grins fast-food stained teeth, his eyes flashing with crazed anticipation in the light of the computer screen, "anything for my brand."

Winter

Treading, stable, I maintain my buoyancy.

Calm water brings memories of an

August eve

The explosive red sinks into the distant ground blending endlessly to deep purple, finally ebony sprinkled with the first stars, silver stratosphere

Baking pavement radiates still

Wide fluorescent pools move in parallels over the arches

Echoing laughter wanes, distant summer

Clicking of gears spent miles in the sun soon to go dormant through deep cold

The boy watches in anticipation for distant spring

Thoughts of endings,

waves begin.

loss...

My father is in the drawer

Put there to remember

The paper, The picture

The hair

The relics not forgotten

All that remains

Cold stone is bare I do not see it

But the drawer, in there

A piece of memory.

I do not open it

it sticks in my mind

But sometimes,

I think,

I can hear it.

The echo fades, my mind is chaos.

I tire of the tread, water coming up to my face,

am I drowning?

Darkness invades,

The feckless coward fingers the enter key, launching radioactive projectiles to rain death on billions. "Fake news," he grins fast-food stained teeth, his eyes flashing with crazed anticipation in the light of the computer screen, "anything for my brand."

Panic overwhelms.

I fight to stay afloat,

Can't breathe.

Letting go,

Wretched maw of despair entombs this bludgeoned carapace which, feeble, is limp in the grotesque visage. Shapeless void and spherical teeth, the pit suckles.

Deeper, darker, the water enclosed.

I can breathe?

Remember...

Only a fish whose dreams of man quickly fade,

gladly simple again, I disappear into unanalyzed depths.

Michael Crane
Corona Road

kip looked over his juice glass and said, "Men in Tyvek suits just took the Italian guy from room 101 out the front. He told the desk clerk he felt sick; just like that he's in quarantine."

Normally, the morning conversation at Hotel Timor was full of corny engineer jokes while sunshine waitresses poured fresh local coffee. This day was different. There was a lot of silent thinking. The papaya didn't taste as sweet.

"So, you think the virus will make it to Timor-Leste?" I asked.

"Might be here already. I guess we won't know for sure until the Italian's test results come back." Skip shrugged. "Who knows where they took him for testing." A dapper Timorese waiter hovered for a second before removing my empty plate like a seagull stealing French fries. Skip's calm and steady voice was perfect for his impromptu role as the day's newscaster.

"Corporate called me last night and said they'll fly anyone home who wants to go. Looks like we may have to evacuate in the next 24 hours anyway. Judy is on her way to the airport now. I fly out at 4:00 p.m.

The floor beneath me dropped like a cut rope. The last thing East Timor needed was another virus. It was already crawling with disease, which is why I'd spent a month justifying an overhaul of the capital city's water system.

How could we possibly be packing up and leaving now because of one more disease? Halfway through that thought, I pointed my fork at Skip. "Here in Dili, open sewers line the streets, dumping grounds for human waste and dead carcasses."

Skip laughed. "All this time I thought those canals were Timorese garden plots."

"Yeah. They grow their veggies in a medium of world class parasites, viruses and debilitating pathogens like Dengue fever, malaria, pneumonia, upper respiratory infections, acute dysentery and diarrhea, central nervous system infections, febrile illnesses, tuberculosis. The list goes on."

Skip looked a little deeper into my eyes and remained silent, a cue for me to finish my donor-collaboration elevator speech. "Those sewers are a public health cocktail causing infant death, chronic malnutrition and severe multi-generational stunting in every demographic group and location throughout the country. This is why we came here, Skip. Now we're going to leave because of one more disease?"

Skip sat back like a diplomat ready to inform the leader of the tiny island nation that the U.S. just invaded their beachfront. "Mike, if corporate says leave, then we have to leave."

"What about today's work?" I asked like a tone-deaf cowboy. "I have meetings with Ambassador Freitas at 10:00; at 1:00 I'm meeting the CEO of the investment company building the Sheraton; and the team of household survey enumerators at 3:00."

I felt my mind starting to compartmentalize. I stuffed all the Covid news into the tiniest babushka doll and buried it with the day's work. The next larger doll held my plan to get to those meetings, and finally the largest doll wondered what the temperature of the pool would be for my 5:00 p.m. swim.

Skip dragged me across the mud of reality. "Did you know that guy from room 101, Mike?"

"Not sure, let me check into it." I texted my Italian friend Guido working for the E.U.

He sent me pictures of himself in wonderful quarantine with champagne bottles on ice beside fluffy omelets on fine china. Guido tells me that he rubbed shoulders with that guy from 101 and now Guido is "having the time of this life for the next 14 days in his seaside apartment with his beautiful wife, trying to 'work' when the internet isn't down."

Next text said, "All thanks to this guy." I looked at the attached mugshot, Exhibit 101, and passed it around.

Cindy, our Portuguese counterpart, glimpsed the phone when she sat to join us said, "Oh, I saw him at breakfast almost every day." She pointed to the next table. "He usually sat right there."

I started looking around the dining room, paused, and asked Skip, "Why does everyone suddenly look Italian to me?" He grinned and said a driver would come to take me to my meetings. Then he made arrangements to send an airport shuttle to pick up Ted, who had already left on his 3-day journey to join us before corporate pulled the plug.

*

In the nearly 20 years since gaining independence from Indonesia in 2002, newly liberated Timorese migrated to the capital, Dili, to take part in building their country. Most land title records were destroyed during the revolution, so new arrivals constructed houses wherever they wanted. Some occupied the riversides. Some took to building on mountains too steep for a chairlift. Others built next to family who came before them to the city, who were already squeezed in next to family who had arrived before them. People built houses with any materials they could afford on a minimum wage of $150 per month. They widened makeshift roads by repeatedly driving over goat trails or walking paths. They dug drainage ditches to channel human shit and storm water into the sea. In the end, none of the makeshift urban sprawl could handle the coming flood.

*

Ted had come to fix Dili's water problems. His voice was such a soft cushion that when he spoke people immediately trusted him. He was as humble as a hyphen; still, you don't become lead infrastructure engineer for corporate unless you know your stuff, and by all accounts, Ted's 30-year track record proved that he was the right man for the job. What he was about to see, however, would push him to his limits.

A skeleton crew—me, Ted and Cindy—met for dinner that evening. Cindy read to us from her phone. "The virus is spreading rapidly around the world. Every hour the death count goes up. South Korea is exploding. Italy is in lock down. Australia is starting to cancel flights. It's finally reached the U.S."

Cindy was a walking Rolodex, indispensable for all things practical. She had an answer for every question. I never knew her official title or training, but it didn't matter because without her nothing got done. She'd been staying at the hotel so long she didn't need a menu. I let her order my meal. Ted ordered the grilled fish special and shared a good bottle of Portuguese wine.

I heard what sounded like static coming from outside. "What's that noise?" I asked. It was like we were in a giant radio that had no reception. When the waitstaff stopped work to stare through the hotel's glass doors, I decided to investigate. "It's raining really hard out there," I reported.

Cindy had seen it rain like that before, or thought she had, and turned back to the daily corona virus news. "Portugal may close its borders next week."

The rain soon turned biblical and dominated everything. The air in the restaurant was noticeably moist; waitstaff stopped working; the lights flickered. Drenched visitors filled the lobby, charging their cell phones at every available outlet. Staff had to mop the red ceramic floor tiles because of all the dripping clothes. It was like an entire wedding party got pushed into the pool, climbed out and ran into the dance hall. Yellow caution signs warned you not to slip and fall.

I stepped toward the portico. A crisp-tailored, 5-foot tall Timorese doorman wearing polished shoes and a gold trimmed bellman hat held the door as if this was any other day. But it wasn't. Power was out across the city. Car horns clamored, generators rumbled, and the deafening rain pounded Dili. The hotel manager and I watched taxis and motorbikes roll past the hotel, water covering most of their wheels.

"I've been here 10 years," said the manager, "and I have never seen the water this high before."

Across the road, we watched a Viking-sized man navigate the traffic, his pants rolled up to his knees, shoes in hand, hunched like someone avoiding a spray of bullets. He waded through the water and up the ramp to the hotel, spoke with Cindy in Portuguese. The hotel manager, Ted and I took videos of the downpour with our phones. Ted contemplated how to fix the drainage that caused the streets to flood.

I was dumbfounded by the amount of water that fell from the sky in just a few hours. If the water is knee deep at the hotel, I realized, then the flood prone areas of the city are getting devastated. I felt like a rubbernecker kneeling over a crash victim. This was not a natural wonder, and I shouldn't have been marveling at hydrology; I should have been concerned about loss of life and property, the very reasons we came to Dili. Moisture in sheets, like a visit to Niagara Falls, found its way under the portico. We returned to the lobby. The doorman grinned as a bankrupt parent might smile at his child on Christmas, and I wondered if he'd just lost his house.

We wove our way through a lobby of charger cables and legs and found four chairs under a giant wall-hanging of colorful Timorese textiles. Cindy introduced us to the barefoot Viking, Bruno. Bruno had a devouring handshake and spoke proficient English. He said he lived and worked in Oecusse, the site of the first Portuguese settlers 500 years ago. Timor honors Oecusse much the same way America reveres Plymouth Rock. Bruno helped build the roads, sidewalks, and airport there.

"Oecusse …" he lilted, his eyes glowing, looking up; his hands followed. "… is so beautiful." He spoke of Oecusse like a vacation home. "Oecusse." Every consonant enunciated slowly and clearly, his tone that of the Lion King announcing the arrival of Simba. "The water is pure," he said. "The oceans give us fresh fish every day. The sand is a carpet. The roads and sidewalks are flawless. All the shops have excellent Portuguese wine. Oecussi has everything you need." Bruno, a bear of a man with a butterfly's

soul, loved his family, loved life, and loved Oecusse. He invited me to visit, and based on his description, I would have been a fool to say no.

Bruno also came bearing news. "Portugal is closing its borders," he said with a lost face.

Cindy's prediction came 7 days early. She quickly decided to leave the next morning or risk not being able to return home.

I felt like someone just stole my computer. When Cindy goes, I won't know how to do anything.

Ted's phone rang. "Corporate calling at this hour?" he said, walking away with puzzled look.

While Ted was gone, Bruno gave an update on the Italian from room 101. "He was taken to isolation like the WHO protocol suggests. East Timor's version of isolation, however, is a shipping container." His jolly demeaner turned somber. "They took him to the port at the edge of the city and locked him in a container with a plastic bag for a toilet. He wasn't in there too long before the neighbors started stoning his container and his police guards. They demanded their neighborhood not become a leper colony for the corona virus. The violence was uncontrollable. Police were forced to remove the patient, and he was flown to Australia for quarantine."

The next morning, I found Cindy in the lobby with her carry-on. Covid protocol had rearranged the dining room. It reminded me of a hotel that's just opened for the first time and didn't have enough furniture. The distance between tables was three times that of yesterday, and the breakfast buffet was spread out over the room. Smiles on the faces of waitstaff were so constrained that it looked like it hurt. Outside, the sun beat down brightly. All the water was gone, trash and mud covered the streets.

"So you're really leaving huh?" I asked Cindy.

The woman who I relied on for advice, nodded and said, "Yes, and you should leave too. Covid is spreading very quickly. Borders around the world are closing without notice. Transiting through countries on the way home may cause you to be delayed. Or you could be turned back. The U.S. just closed its borders to all flights from Europe. Mike, there are only three ways out of Timor, either through Singapore, Darwin, or Bali, and

Singapore closed yesterday. Darwin will close in two days."

I was stunned and replied, "Well, Bali is nice." I slipped pineapple into my mouth just as Ted walked in with his suitcase "Not you too?!" I shouted.

"Corporate is closing all projects worldwide and repatriating all employees," he explained. "It's not just us. All international engineering firms are going home. The State Department is sending most of its employees home. The Peace Corps is expatriating all volunteers, and the U.S. is threatening to close its borders." He stirred his coffee. "When is your flight?"

"I'm scheduled to depart in 7 days. I've got a lot of work to do before I go."

Cindy looked at me like somebody'd broken my toys. "Mike, the flood has destroyed President Guterres' office. The government is shutting down. There are over 5,000 displaced people in neighborhoods directly behind this hotel. The hospital's only emergency room was destroyed. The statistics office where you were supposed to go today is completely flooded, many records are destroyed. If you didn't get a call yet, you will after they get the cell towers working again. I am sure your meetings are cancelled." A polished black SUV, Hotel Timor in gold letters on the side, pulled up to the front door. "That's our airport shuttle, Mike, got to go." A porter took their Samsonites. Cindy checked her phone one last time, "Looks like New York is America's hotspot right now, 2,382 are infected. The number of new cases doubled from yesterday."

I felt like we were walking in a funeral procession out to the airport shuttle. "Take care of yourself Mike." Ted extended his warm hand.

"Cindy?" I begged for one last bit of data. "How many cases in East Timor?"

"None." she smiled, as if reading my mind. The car door closed. I saw my face reflecting in the black glass, alone, the sun heating my back.

An overstuffed lobby couch swallowed me whole. I ordered a coffee and watched tourists check out of the hotel. The international aid community had set up a makeshift flood response center in one corner. My thoughts ran barefoot on a hockey pond chasing truth from home to Timor and back.

What is my next move? I took an inventory. I am healthy. My daughter is in Brooklyn, the Covid epicenter. Is she safe? No cases in East Timor yet but many people are hurting from flood devastation. I came here to help stop the flooding and fix the waterborne disease problem. My colleagues were directed to evacuate at a most critical and informative time. Because I am a private sub-contractor, I am under no such directive, but if I don't leave soon, I could be stranded here. I need the future now to come crashing through the plate glass windows and tell me what to do. I should do something.

I headed toward the front door before my coffee arrived and started walking toward a dust cloud hovering in the distance; I guessed helicopters had just landed. I grabbed the first taxi and directed him east toward the dust. A whistle-happy policeman soon diverted my taxi because of a bridge threatening to collapse. Pedestrians swarmed in conflicting directions and blocked our way. As we inched through the snarl, I saw mud streaked faces of exhaustion, outrage, confusion, helplessness. We moved along at a walking pace with the crowd. Everyone appeared worked and worn, their clothes stained with survival. Faces peered into the taxi to investigate me, an accidental voyeur. Guilt flooded the backseat. I reminded myself that my mission was to understand the flood's impact so that I could make an even stronger case for investing millions of dollars to prevent another tragedy. The faces scrutinizing me didn't know that. They were hungry, but the flood had destroyed the food markets. They were thirsty, but the water was muddy.

What is the value of tomorrow when today has departed?

To my right, dozens of people shoveled dirt and pushed wheelbarrows in a large family compound. On the left, a Honda minivan, windows blown out, sat filled to the dashboard with muck, tree limbs, dish rags, a plastic toy lawn mower, and chunks of dinnerware protruding. The sound of generators was slanderous. People yelled to be heard over the racket.

Turning the corner, I saw the only white person I would come across on my damage tour. A nun in front of a Catholic mission removed a broken bed frame from the walkway. A long line of mothers with babies and elderly waiting to get inside the mission. The flood had covered everything in silt for the sun to bake into dust. Dust was mushrooming over half of the city as people swept and dug their way back home. Dust was the grand equalizer. The driver and I started to cough uncontrollably. People on the street covered their mouths with dusty rags, shirt collars, their hands, some with nothing. I saw a mother using her only free hand to cover the mouth of her baby. A hunched elderly man seemed reconciled to his fate.

The dust settled so thickly that street signs were illegible. A house-sized pile of trash diverted us again, this time down a mud road. The taxi tires struggled for grip. The driver remained silent as we navigated over rutted alleyways.

After an hour, seeing hundreds of destroyed homes, I directed the driver back to the hotel. I sank into the backseat and noticed the car rolling down smooth pavement again. I felt like the last person to board a plane just before they closed the door.

Where was the national guard, the rescue workers, the ambulances? I've only seen one policeman. Where was the international aid community? Did they all leave because of the corona virus? Or were they in the hotel "planning" a response? How useless am I? What is the purpose of international aid when thousands are left homeless and aid workers fly home because of a virus?

My eyes closed and the taxi became an armored car blocking out all violence and viruses, destruction and disease. Maybe I was safe, but I was alone, shoved out onto an empty dance floor, the rest of the world behind plate glass, watching me, placing bets on what I'd do next. I felt tears well up and did not know why.

The taximan politely woke me. "Sixteen dollars please." I paid and exited.

The doorman seemed to have a pocketful of apropos grins, this one was a poignant, "I told you so." I took a seat in the same leather couch and ordered another coffee. The waiter asked with a wink and smile, "Would you like the last one we made for you or a fresh one?"

I thought, how are the Timorese able to smile at all? Bruno saw me from across the lobby and made his way past the life-size wooden carvings of warriors with spears to take a seat next to me. He said, "You look like your dog died."

"Half the city is destroyed from a flood we were working to prevent. And when it happens, we all leave because of a virus that isn't here yet. I'm the last person from my team and I have 7 more days before I leave. What can I do here alone? I'm not an engineer. And what can an economist possibly do now besides help shovel dirt. Then I see all around me smiling Timorese who seem to ignore what just happened. There isn't a single emergency worker anywhere near the flood site. Everyone I talk to wants me to go home. Does anyone care?" I poured my consciousness onto the coffee table.

Bruno looked at me as if consoling a grandson after his first breakup. "Mike, the reason there are no cases in Timor is because there is no testing being done. This country has no ability, no resources, and no trained professionals to test for a virus spreading like wildfire across the globe. People from China and South Korea are flying in and out of Dili every day. The virus is probably all over this hotel lobby right now. I am leaving in the morning for Oecusse. There are very few people there. We have a compound with plenty of room and enough food and wine for six months. You should come. You can have your own room, the internet works great, and the beach is right across the road."

*

The airport was quiet at 6:00 a.m. because the usual mass of taxi drivers and trinket hawkers were still sleeping. A small commuter airline serving only Oecusse made one round-trip each morning, except Sunday. Bruno and I stepped up to a battered but functional counter. We each bought a one-way ticket. A teenager in a Michael Jackson tee-shirt weighed our luggage on a bathroom scale and then weighed each of us before guiding us outside and across the tarmac, where porters loaded the belly of the plane with cargo, food supplies, and mail.

The co-pilot turned in her seat with her headset above her ears. "The emergency exit is over there," she barked, "and everyone must wear their seatbelt. We will arrive in Oecusse in 35 minutes. Enjoy your flight." With that, the propellers started whacking air and the plane bumped to the end of the runway. For the next 35 minutes I was given a tour of Timor's beautiful coastline, steep mountains, lush green and deep blues.

Company pickup trucks shuttled us to Bruno's compound. The first person I met was Santiago, Director of Operations for the Oecusse project. Trimmed and tanned, handsome and friendly, Santiago introduced me to his beautiful wife, Amanda, a blond whose face said, "I love fun." They welcomed me like a prodigal son. After showing me my room, we all went immediately to the beach bar across the road. Amanda ordered a giant gin and tonic; Santiago ordered a cold beer. It was 9:30 a.m. and I hadn't eaten breakfast yet, so I ordered a coffee and an omelet. The bar owner took a sympathetic look at me like I might be ill.

Over breakfast, Bruno, Santiago, Amanda, and their friend Clarissa discussed my fate. Santiago said, "The virus is likely in Timor, but we can't confirm. We assume it is, and we take all necessary precautions. This is a safe place to wait out the pandemic. Very few people come and go from Oecusse. You can stay here and be safe. Go home when it all dies down."

I pondered out loud, "If I am going to shelter in place, then why do it here? Shouldn't I go home?"

Amanda said, "Portugal's borders are closing today. We can't go home. Even if I could go, I would not be able to help my family. Looks like we are all on our own. The safest place for you is here. New York has 1,000 more confirmed cases from just yesterday."

I nodded. "And my flight lands in JFK."

"We are having a party tonight, lets enjoy the day while you think about it," Santiago concluded with a big smile.

That evening Bruno grilled a fish bigger than my leg; he grilled lobsters, and pork ribs, and steak. The coolers were full of every drink imaginable. An entire table was full of enough liquor bottles to rival the best bar in New Orleans. Karaoke started and the Timorese came to life with their natural talent for singing. When they struggled with the words to a Creedence Clearwater Revival song, I jumped in to save them. When the bad moon arose at midnight, we all walked across the road and jumped in the warm, moonlit Savu Sea. The party wilted a natural death and I retired to my room, washed off the salt and got under the covers. I saw the moon peaking though the window and I thought of my daughter who was moving out of her Brooklyn college dorm to finish her semester

on-line at home. I thought of my family. *Should I be partying when a global pandemic is threatening. What if food supplies start to dwindle, what if water supplies are threatened. Will my family be able to survive? They might need me. What if someone I love gets sick and I am unable to fly home?*

In the morning I drank my coffee on the beach and watched fishermen who had been working for hours. The sun warmed my body. Santiago came and brought the morning news. "Mike, in 2 days the Bali airport will prohibit all entry to foreigners without a heath certificate that says you are Covid free. Timor's hospital is basically destroyed and getting that certificate will be almost impossible. Your ticket is through Bali. You can't change to Singapore or Darwin because they already closed, and there is no other air route out of here. I heard on CNN that the U.S. is requesting all citizens to return home or risk being quarantined in place for a lengthy and unknown time. As I said yesterday, we are happy to have you as our guest until this is over, but if you are thinking of going home, then you have only 2 days to get to Bali. Today is Sunday, and there are no flights to Dili today."

I grumbled in my lowest tone, "Well this a far cry from the whiskey-toting, skinny-dipping playboy I saw last night." We both absorbed the peaceful silence of the morning sun, listened to waves chime, and finished our coffee.

"Can you get me on tomorrow's flight to Dili?" I asked.

He replied, "I'll check the availability this evening when they open."

I calculated my travel plans out loud. "So, I need to land in Bali before midnight tomorrow night or they will send me back here, right?"

"Right" Santiago nodded.

"My flight home from there leaves 5 days later through Doha. Is Doha still open?"

"I think so" he said.

I asked him to text Cindy. "She'll know faster than anyone. Then from Doha I fly to JKF and sit in the airport for 8 hours before connecting to Burlington. And JFK is polluted with Covid."

Santiago added, "If the U.S. borders are even open, they seem to be threatening to close."

"So, if I can't get a seat on this little 30-minute commuter flight tomorrow then all of these connections are meaningless, and I'll be moving in with you."

"Hey, it could be worse." Santiago said. He got up, brushed off the sand and walked back to the house.

I strolled down the beach and thought about how I had lost all control over my life. *There is truly little I can do about any of this but hate knowing it.* I started to wonder if I ever had any control over anything. *How did I get on this tiny island? Am I even my own person? Am I me because of the choices I made, or am I merely collateral damage from a long series of disconnected events? Am I on this beach as an environmental economist, former Peace Corps volunteer, carpenter, college graduate, father of two, burning under the Timor sun because I chose my future? Or is this what chaos actually looks like? Maybe everything that happens to us is imposed by invisible forces and the decisions we make are only illusions of comfort to prevent us from going insane.*

I was a mile away from the compound, wandering an abandoned beach. The fishermen were hiding from the noonday sun. The heat created waves in the air like a toaster does before it serves breakfast. I was burning, thirsty, and there were no witnesses. I waded knee deep in the water wondering if I could float home. A nubile mermaid surfaced and asked me if I wanted to go snorkeling. She handed me a mask. I took it and followed her lead. I saw clouds of bright blue fish sparkle in the sun. I saw a lone puffer fish with menacing spikes, a florescent octopus, and tiny, helpless, pink seahorses being pushed by the ocean, seemingly content at their lack of control. A majestic dugong then effortlessly finned past me as if to test my courage. I froze in amazement; she swam so slowly but was gone in seconds. I fell in love with the lack of oxygen.

I returned to the compound and regrouped with the others around a dining table filled with a bounty of leftovers. Bruno poured his favorite wine. Before my first bite, Santiago said "Mike, I'm sorry but the flight to Dili tomorrow is completely sold out." Everyone looked for my reaction. I thought about the seahorses.

"Call the Flight Director and tell him to send another plane and I'll pay for all 17 seats," I said.

Understanding my resolve, Santiago excused himself to try and make contact on a Sunday evening. We were all satiated from last night's festivities; we sat and told stories for a while and went to bed early.

In the morning, I was packed and ready to go by 7:00 a.m. My newfound Portuguese family stood in solidarity with my mission and hugged me goodbye. Bruno and I counted 17 passengers climb the four steps into the plane, not one no-show. We knocked on the Director's office and Bruno opened the door before a reply. The Director was already on the phone debating with Santiago that another plane cost more than just 17 seats. Each take-off and landing costs airport fees, taxes, and overtime salary. Bruno cried bunk while I stood silently in the corner. The director made no commitment and we left before the police escorted us out.

On the way back to the compound, I stuck my head out the window and let the wind scrape my face. Amanda and Clarissa welcomed me back with bigger hugs than when I left. Santiago was on the phone, his conversation energized; he paced the floor. I didn't understand a word of his Portuguese, but I got the gist. After 45 minutes he hung up. "I managed to commandeer another flight," he said. "Be ready for noon."

If I arrived in Dili by 1:00 p.m. then maybe I'll be able to reschedule my flight to Bali, which can only be done in-person at the airport. The chances are slim that there'll be an extra seat since it's the last flight out before Indonesia closes its borders.

We said goodbye again, like in "Groundhog Day". My expressions of gratitude were inadequate for the occasion. I invited them all to my next Thanksgiving dinner and mounted the truck. Bruno parked in the fire lane and walked me to the gate. I thanked him for everything and promised we would see each other again.

I landed at Dili airport with a mission to get on the next flight to Bali, departing in three hours. The airport was crowded with people making deals, dogs yelping, pop music at inappropriate volume, officials barking orders that no one heeded, and lots of on-lookers doing nothing but watching everyone else. Keeping my place in line required a firm stance. I got to the window and found a body oozing with indifference. I asked, "Can I change this ticket to Bali for the next flight?"

"Haven't you heard?" the woman said without expression. "There was an earthquake in Bali."

My mind split in two. On the left side, my heart stopped. I wanted to break down. My right side responded without missing a beat. "Will the plane leave on time?"

I barely heard the woman over the mayhem of the airport. "I am not sure if it's leaving but, in any case, I think the flight is full. Let me check. Can I have your ticket please?"

During my 20-minute wait I was solicited to buy a key chain made from woven bamboo, a hot dog in puff pastry, a cassette tape that allegedly contained romantic Timorese music, and a florescent orange drink of unknown origin.

The ticket agent returned and asked for my passport without making eye contact. She turned away and I heard the printer chirping. She turned back and handed me a boarding pass. "Gate One."

"Wait what? What, what about the earthquake?" my left brain couldn't believe I actually held a ticket to Bali in my hands.

"Six-point-two on the scale. They are monitoring for a Tsunami now. Good luck in Bali. Next please."

I found my fellow passengers self-isolating in the waiting area so I used the airport Wi-Fi to book a room at an airport hotel in Bali. As soon as arrived, I planned to go to the Qatar Airways office to change my original New York flight for the next morning.

The plane arrived from Bali and almost no one got off. It sat on the runway for an hour before we started boarding, we, the lucky travelers on the last flight out of Timor without restrictions, but it didn't feel that way. The line moved silently; our Corona masks more like gags. I felt as if we were in a grey-toned dystopian movie shuffling into a mineshaft.

The flight was completely full. I refused the food service and stared at the ocean for the duration of the 55-minute flight wondering if I could have kayaked to Bali. Upon arrival, immigration officials questioned me about my travels. Somebody took my temperature and I was cleared to enter.

I rolled my luggage through the viscera of Bali's tourism industry: an open-air market for guided tours, hotels on remote beaches, sim cards, and phone credit. I continued through the pecking order of taxi drivers and into my hotel lobby.

"Your room is ready, Mr. Crane," said a handsome Balinese front desk clerk with a smile. After asking, he told me the location of the Qatar Airways office and arranged a taxi to take me there. Things were working out—I thought—*I made the right decision to come to this hotel. I'm finally in control again.*

A moonfaced taximan in a blue flowered shirt waited to drive me to Qatar Airways, his head wrapped in a colorful turban, his smile the size of a catcher's mitt.

"Normally there would be traffic jams here, but all the tourists have gone home. You are my only customer this week," he lamented.

I wasn't listening; my thoughts vacillated between feelings of desperation and self-control. As we drove up to the office, I felt like an addicted gambler about to place everything I owned on one roll. I asked the taximan to wait.

A security guard checked my temperature and allowed me inside. What I saw next was reminiscent of a New York City unemployment office during the depression. I wanted to tell my taximan that had I found all of his missing tourists in the Qatar Airways office.

The air conditioner was overworked and underperforming. A young couple sweated over paperwork with a broken pen. The blonde had hundreds of licorice-sized braids that pulled her forehead skin and exposed a florescent white scalp. Her boyfriend looked like he barely survived a tsunami but not without hauling out a bounty of sea kelp.

A lone black woman on the verge of tears talked to one of the three available agents. A couple with a British accent bickered politely about the virtues of sequestering in Bali. I did nothing but stare at the mayhem. After 15 minutes of standing in the bustle, an official looking woman asked me in a crispy Russian accent, "Can I help you?"

I said, "I have a flight to New York in 5 days and I would like to change it to tomorrow. I understand from an email that there is no fee for changing?"

She looked at me like I was the 87th lost soul she'd seen that day and said, "This office is only for redirecting cancelled flights. Has your flight been cancelled?"

"No."

"You still have a confirmation for your flight to New York?"

"Yea?" My voice drooped.

"Then the only way you can make a change is on-line."

By this time, twenty people, three rows deep, were peering into my space to grasp any shred of information that might help them. I felt like a union representative negotiating on the picket line. I explained that I'd already tried the website and received several error messages stating that the changes can't be made. "That is the only way, there is nothing I can do here, you have to keep trying."

Back in my hotel I tried the website again. They were allowing changes and a few seats were still available.

Success! I'm back in control.

I clicked "pay" and saw the price: $9,000. I thought I selected first class by accident, but no, economy class now cost 10 times the normal price.

So much for Covid sympathy.

I shriveled, crushed again by my inability to direct my own path. After sulking for an hour my ego took over again. I restarted my computer, pulled out my credit card and prepared to pay nine-grand just to make a point.

Enter confirmation number.

Click "change ticket" and select date.

And nothing. Not only is the $9,000 ticket gone, but there were no seats available at any price.

I'm stranded in Indonesia for the next 5 days. But will it only be five?

CNN was blasting on the hotel TV. U.S. borders would close soon. New York is locked down; 500 deaths in 1 day. Indonesia is closed. Qatar is closed to tourists, though the airport is still open. I realized that there was more at risk than being stranded for 5 days.

There was a danger greater than the U.S. closing its borders. The loss of money and convenience was nothing compared to the loss of my own identity. Every bit of who I believed I was slowly crumbled under the weight of an abstraction. An invisible drain was sucking me down into a world that I hadn't created, a world that I had no choice except to enter and endure whatever lay in store for me.

I am at risk of losing the concept of self, myself. What remains on the black side of the unknown frightens me. Stranded in Bali for 5 days ... I started to shiver.

*

The jungle road ended unexpectedly at a perpendicular cow path. My moonfaced driver had stopped smiling after his GPS died. We climbed a hill to look for the retreat. At the top we found a rolling sea of giant green rectangles molding over each other like greedy fingers. "I think the retreat's east in those rice patties." I guessed but didn't really care. Three prayers and a cigarette later my driver took a left turn between two dinosaur-sized statutes of Buddha, then through another half-mile of rice fields. I've never been to this strange land and had no idea what to expect.

At the orientation house, I surrendered my cell phone, street clothes, and shoes. I washed, put on a cotton robe and checked in for 72 hours of silence.

My three-sided room, with a bed, overlooked over the jungle. I closed the door and sat. Green whistles and song trees and water touched the air with empty lungs. Time percolated into the soil and reincarnated into palm fronds and banana leaves and mice. The jungle gaggled a haunted orchestra of sounds that drew me out the door and down a foot path. I found the 106 Steps of Contemplation and started to descend, stopping for a prayer on each landing, down to the river's edge, to the Crying Bench.

I sat and felt my skin shrink. My throat tightened. My face contorted and tears dropped. I cried for the lost souls who knew me before I ever did. I cried for my daughter's forthcoming world. I cried for the rice farmers hinged to this land. I cried for my son born too soon. Tears rained down. I wailed. My nose was slick. I cried for the altruism that had left me decades earlier. I cried for my charade. I cried about the façade I had built to survive in a throat-slit world. I cried for my mistaken marriage and drifted lover. *Will she ever care?*

My robe was soiled; I was on my knees. I wailed for help. I cried over my chains of loneliness. I cried for more silence. I wept as control dripped through my fingers. I grieved over my own death.

*

Three days later, the meditation gong echoed as usual at 5:00 a.m. My new world, 4 hours away at the Bali airport, awaited me. Time to go home.

I accept the virus that plagues our world and I accept the unknown. But will my country accept me?

Three days of silence has passed without CNN, without body counts, or bodies.

Are the gates open, will the planes fly?

Bouncing through the last rice fields, I relinquished any illusion of control.

I am neither a carpenter nor an economist, but a fragment of time. I did not create a family; but was given one. I cannot save the flooded Timorese any more than I can stop a virus from spreading. I do not serve a lost people with solutions; I only returned what I was given. My flights will depart if the sun heats, the oceans cool and the winds rise. Home will welcome me.

I reached into my pocket for a grin but that's a skill reserved for doormen. My emotions now came from the shadows of the morning sun. I found my cell phone, thought about powering on, but instead dropped it into the bottom of my backpack. I gazed out the window and wondered if the arc in the rice farmer's back will ever straighten.

Janet Preus

My House Is on Fire, But I'm Not in It

ne day, my daughter called me and said, "I don't want to work anymore." She's in the Army in the midst of teaching at the JAG school, so she's not in a position to quit, nor would she. But I know what she means, and I answer, "That's funny. I don't, either." In fact, the day before she called, I had stopped mid-sentence in an article I was editing, marched downstairs where my Significant Other has set up a makeshift office, and announced, "I don't want to work anymore." Moot point, in my case, as well. S.O. just looked at me, no surprise on his face. He'd be blissfully happy fully retired doing nothing at all. But I'm a not-enough-hours-in-the-day kind of personality.

We had not had a single person in our house since the night before my brother-in-law's funeral. The day after his funeral, the church was closed, as was almost everything else, as the realities of the pandemic slammed against our collective grief. That was in early March. This was June.

Friends and writing colleagues say they, too, are having trouble concentrating, getting anything done, or even caring if they do. Happy hours on zoom.com are spent talking about how we're not happy. We are all coming to understand separation from a larger pattern, a rhythmic cycle that can be relied upon, like holidays or a school year. We have no beginning, no middle, no end. Get up, work, hope it's nice enough to get outside, eat something, look at the clock, go back to work, look at the clock, watch the news, which is always the same news. Load the dishwasher. Look at the clock again, which says 8:30 p.m. and wonder, "Can I go to bed yet?"

The answer is, "No." Unless you want to be up at midnight with nothing but your thoughts clogged with every stupid thing you've ever done, every horrid mistake, every mediocre guy you've slept with, every dollar you spent unwisely, every careless comment you ever made, every time you drank too much …

But go ahead. Crawl into bed with a book that reminds you that yours isn't published yet and get whatever sleep you can. The isolation, the conscientiously staying at home … periods of peace, a burst of joy, then a strange sort of suspension devoid of any deep emotional content. You are just … there. You sense incremental change, barely perceptible moment to moment, but, like growing older, increasingly obvious over the long term.

*

I'd love to FaceTime with my granddaughter, but she's on Zoom for school, or on Facetime with her friends, and I don't want her having that much screen time. Meanwhile, she's getting older—incrementally, almost imperceptibly day by day. And so am I. So, I call, but her parents don't pick up. They need to get away from their devices, too.

Rather than work, write, call family, or plant herbs, I'll look at this tree, watch the birds landing on its branches and see if I can figure out which one is singing which song. I'll dig my fingers in the dirt in my little flower bed. I hear nothing but the birds calling out for a mate in the yard, the puttering of a small motorboat on the lake, or just a faint breeze that makes the leftover oak leaves clackity clack together. Just that. For the moment, that's perfect.

If my neighbor starts any one of his motorized tools or pieces of machinery, including that goddam lawnmower, I may lose it. It's hard enough to concentrate on birds. Or dirt.

When it's quiet—so quiet that the motorboat is out of hearing, the neighbor has put away his power tools, and the breeze has dwindled to nothing so the lake is as flat as a giant mirror—I think, "I guess I'm fine." The patterns, rhythms, cycles of life that we rely on are still there. They must be. They're just lurking in the background, waiting until it's safe to come out.

I am able to live at my cabin in the north woods. I should feel lucky, but it's not what I want. I don't want to reach that point yet. I don't want to be old, incrementally or otherwise. I want to be a dynamo, breezing through my stack of creative writing projects, dashing off to a workshop, a writing session, or rehearsal of one of my plays. Instead, I'm sitting on my deck, cradling my second (or is it my third?) glass of wine, the energy leaking from my cells, evaporating off my shirt, slithering across the boards and sprinkling themselves on the pine needles below. Gone. I have melted into this existential confusion caused by a pandemic. We have no playbook for it. Not that I'd read it. Takes too much energy.

This weird global health crisis has convinced me to not call people any more (because I'm technology weary), not throw dinner parties, (can't, too risky), not go to church (there is no church, except on Zoom and I'm technology weary, so … can't). In short, I have permission to let go of a lot of things I thought I wanted to do, and which now seem burdensome.

If we have anything to gain longer term from this, maybe it is the forced pause that made us interested in birds calling, in watching leaves bud out, in hearing the wind make dry oak leaves crackle.

*

Then, a man named George Floyd was killed by a police officer in Minneapolis and the empty, patternless, quiet void that felt so peculiar became the subject of wistful longing.

My S.O. and I own the downstairs of a big, old house in the heart of the city I love. I haven't lived there since February. The malaise I have been feeling now seems overwhelmingly self-indulgent, and I give in to crying. Anything or nothing makes me cry. The news, a phone call from my daughter, a baby crawling around in a diaper commercial. The void—the emptiness—is now tangible. Thousands have marched past my favorite neighborhood restaurants, boarded up. They shouted for justice, and the pandemic be damned.

A much uglier dynamic flared up in just hours and took down the life of Lake Street, a street that's been part of the city as long as it's been a city:

The K-Mart where I biked to get garden gloves and potting soil.

The post office where I mailed my kids' Christmas presents.

The Wells Fargo where I banked when I first got to know this neighborhood.

The Office Depot where I copied scripts of my plays.

The Walgreens where I bought shampoo and lotion.

Still, what's that? All are part of much larger entities that will make decisions someplace far away, swoop in and recover what can be recovered, rebuild, or leave the rest for another large entity to decide about. I think of the smaller, locally owned businesses damaged or gone altogether:

My nail salon that used to be run by a young Ethiopian woman.

The family owned Scandinavian import shop where I browsed with my daughter, planning her wedding.

The jewelry store that repaired the mother's ring my children gave me.

*

Our beloved local musicians, the Steeles, set up a Facebook "Concert for Healing" on Jevetta Steele's front lawn. Their brand of soul, R&B and Gospel has me dancing, singing along and crying some more. "Hold On" they sing in gorgeous harmony.

"Yes, hold on, Minneapolis! Hold on!" I holler at my computer.

Jearlyn breaks down in loud sobs in the middle of "My Prayer." Billy picks it up with a keyboard solo until she toughs her way through to the end. I'm sobbing, too.

But why am *I* crying? I'm not hurt, threatened personally or afraid for my life. I have work, I have food, I have a safe place to eat, sleep, write and rest. I can't explain why I can't stop crying, just like I can't stop crying. I don't think I have a right to be crying all the time, and that makes me cry, too.

Perhaps I am mourning in a way I have never mourned. I lost my parents to old age. It was peaceful. I lost my oldest and best friend. I still cry about her years later. That's life, that's death. I mourned. But not like this.

I am incapable of understanding this.

My House—my neighborhood, my city, my country and my world, this whole big house—is on fire, and I am not in it. I'm watching waves crash on a shore lined with cedar trees while neighbors I know and those I don't know figure out how to get groceries with all the stores looted or damaged. While my writing partner, Fred Steele, and his family sing about bringing people together in love, I am utterly absent. I've always been absent from the turmoil and fear people of color know.

There is a world reeling in pain out there while I have been listening to oak leaves crackle and birds calling. Tomorrow I will get in the car and drive the 200 miles back to my city home.

The images in the news could not have prepared me for what I saw, much less what I felt. I don't live on the east end of Lake Street—the part where the violence took off, where the AutoZone was set ablaze and the 3rd precinct was abandoned and torched. Chicago and 38th Street where George Floyd was killed isn't my neighborhood, either, although it's an easy bike ride from mine. Mounds of flowers, now wilted, obscured the names written on the street by the time I got there.

But my neighborhood—Nicollet's Eat Street, and Lyndale from the Wedge Coop to West Lake Street, and Lake all the way to Hennepin and beyond—was a fortress of fresh plywood and particle board, mostly painted over with spectacular street art proclaiming "I can't breathe," "Say his name," and "Justice for George."

Except for the buildings that were completely gone. A pit of charred ruins as if a tiny bomb had dropped on just that one, small, aging brick building, leaving its neighboring building untouched—equally old and nondescript. A black, deep hole with nothing at all to salvage. Nothing. So completely destroyed it had lost the scent of fire. I couldn't stop staring at the hole, or the hole across the street, both on Chicago Avenue next to the bridge over the greenway I had biked so many times.

My city … my "house" … had had a brush with war; it had been on fire, and *my* problem was lethargy! The risk of a virus that could kill me floated above the humid haze that draped over the windless summer street and dissipated. For the moment, I didn't think of it. For a little while, a single life—a man I certainly didn't know—became more important, and I was done crying

Dan Butterfass
Sweat Lodge

5:15

Inside Dan Abraham Healthy Living Center
Men's steam room the atmosphere's
A sweat lodge
Where I'm naked among
Members of my tribe

5:16

The patterned tiles gleam
Pastels polished
Smooth as river stones
Six walls facing our six
Sacred directions dripping
In beaded condensation
A hot steady rain
Of fine droplets
The scalding
Cairn of river rocks
Long since removed
(For the sake of safety)
From the center of the floor
Replaced by stainlesssteel drain
The source of our sacred
Fire beyond a mysterious
Vent now issuing a hissing spume
Of geyserhot steam each time our sacred
Firekeeper concealed in a utility
Closet beyond the south wall pours
With a hollowed-out wooden scoop
Cold piped riverwater we hear scorch
The pulsing red heat of the stones

5:19

A long continuous hiss
And moan of steam in fissures
That last until our tireless
Firekeeper out of pity finally halts
The barrage with a sudden

Automatic click
As if our steam is set on a timer
A mechanized switch that ushers in
A deep primordial hush
Dense floor-to-ceiling whorls
So thick I can only make out the faintest
Outline of members of my tribe
An apparition of faces
That shifts in and out of focus
A silence so pure
It's from an ancient time
Before the ancient hymns
Before the ancient choirs
Before even the first word
Spoken by the first man
Steam so thick it stifles breath

5:20

In the hours before dawn we gather
During our lunch breaks we gather
Before and after work we gather
In this pristine heat and fluid
My tribe enduring
The line between pain and pleasure
To float free of our cares
Until one by one as a tribe we emerge
From the amniotic dark
Facing the sun's
Eternal rebirth
Back into the light of the world
As if gasping for first breath
Our skin supple
Infantsoft and new
Tingling as we emerge
From this living symbol
Our Mother Earth's sacred womb

5:23

My tribal brothers
In science and medicine
Come and go
Yet without prayers
Without offerings of tobacco
Or red cedar incense
Without medicine bundles
For we are not Indians
    Not *Mdewakanton*
Not Wahpekute
Not Santee
Not Lakota
Not Hunkpapa
Nevertheless we're not quite
Fully *Wasichus* either
We're almost something
Else, almost something indefinably
Special while immersed in the steam
My tribe's sweat lodge
Almost a true sweat lodge
Except for the dim light
Of incandescent bulbs
Glowing from metal
Safety cages
A digital clock
That displays time's
Harsh red numbers
Brutal tick-tock
So no one stays in too long
So that my tribe of healers
Will always be on time for work
A true sweat lodge
Would be dark as inside a cave
Except for a pulsing cairn of river stones
And tip of the peace pipe as it passes
Hand-to-hand
Like a floating ember

5:26

A true sweat lodge
Would smell of wood
And tobacco smoke

Be round as an image
Of the circle of life
Not square
Not this cube of hard
Edges and lines
Grouted ceramic tile
Its frame woven
Of peeled willow sapling
Bowed and lashed
With deer or bison
Sinew
Wigwam-style
Domed walls
And roof a pungent
Weave of pine
And cedar boughs
Mudded with clay
Cache of moccasins
Outside the swift
Zumbro River current
A barely audible whisper

5:27

And there would not now be circulating in our
    steam
An antiseptic congress of egotism
Nor hubris
Nor arrogance
Nor God Complex
But these are the mark of my tribe
Occupational hazards
Of those doing the near-miraculous
Work of my tribe
Best of the brightest men of medicine
Whose collective genius hour-by-hour
Tips the balance between death and life
Surgeons whose dexterous hands perform
Earthly miracles for this famous Clinic
At great personal risk
Of physician's Black Lung Disease
This big problem among my tribal brethren
To become addicted to the belief
That one knows nearly everything

About almost anything
Such as horses
Such as hunting
Such as native wildflowers
Such as fine art
Such as French wine
Such as classical music
Such as Shakespeare
Nor would my tribal brethren
After they step from the steam
Stare with admiration into mirrors
Overpleased by their own visages
Nor in the privacy of their grand tepees
Treat their squaws as receptacles
For semen and jobstress

5:29

But this is my tribe
This is my tribe with whom for better
And for worse I have lain down my roots
My tribe seeking surcease
From its worries here in the steam
In one of the world's famous places
Where peoples from all ends
Of the earth, from all walks and from every
Nation on earth arrive in jets
In search of healing
Far too many for freedom
From fear of immanent death
Here in this world
Famous mecca for the medical arts
Where people of all creeds and religions
Of all colors and all cultures
Gather in one place
Under one roof mingling
Huddled together in the same waiting rooms
Just as warring tribes in earlier times
Gathered all across the West
Where it was agreed by mutual consent
There would be no fighting
Where there flowed healing waters
Among enemies soaking in mineral pools
At the hot springs

5:31

The Dali Lama was just here
Preaching peace
Many Great Fathers from Washington have
    come here
Hollywood comes here
Lou Gehrig was diagnosed here
Cortisone was discovered here
JFK was here as a teenager for his chronic back
(Cutting—it is still rumored—a wide
Swath through the surfeit of single nurses)
Hemingway was electroshocked just down
And across the street from my house
At the world's largest hospital
Where my wife works
The great author's temples rubbed with grease
His memory swiftly erased
As he bit down on the thick rubber mouthpiece
Gerald Ford came here just before he passed
Ronald Reagan before he loped off
To the Happy Hunting Grounds
Bill Clinton dedicated this shine
Our new employee fitness center
Our tribe's sacred sweat lodge
Charles Lindbergh, Helen Keller, Roy Rogers
FDR at the height of his powers
All guests of the Brothers Mayo
Great Chiefs Will and Charlie
Today's Post-Bulletin says Saudi King
Jumbo jets transporting his entourage
Will soon be landing
At this great and important hub on earth
To which people of great means
Along with the poorest of the poor
Arrive together as refugees and pilgrims
To check into the edifice of our Clinic
Too often as a last desperate search for help
All united by hope
We pray to be healed
By the grace of the Great Spirit
Through the integrated councils
And dance of collective genius
Of my tribe of holy men and women
Amen

5:34

This team of doctors of great renown
All of whom breathe a long sigh
Of release here in the steam
Surgeons mingling with nurses
Chief financial officers with orderlies
All seeking respite from the weight
Of their cares in the purifying
Heat of the steam
Relief from the invisible
Pall that hangs like an inversion
In the air over the shallow valley of my tribe
Fine particulates
Soot of death and disease
Settling in our lungs like coal dust

5:36

We let it seep from our pores
Here in the steam
We purge ourselves
Here in the steam
We build up a little immunity
Here in the steam
Before we step out
From the sanctuary of our sweat lodge
Back into the trenches
Of our species' long and ongoing
War without beginning or end
My tribe of healers having counted
Coup many times on our enemies
My tribe of warriors having won
Many skirmishes since our forebears
Broke this prairie sod
My tribe of innovators having forged
New kinds of weaponry and armor
A logo of three overlapping shields
Patient Care
    Education
      Research
In order that we might
Lose this war ever more slowly
So that those already cut down
As our tribe's great shaman once thundered

Pounding his podium
Shall not have died in vain

5:37

I am in reverie here in the steam
In reverie over my tribe's origins
In reverie over its humble roots
I am proud here in the stream
How this great city rose up
How this sprawling campus rose up
From nothing
From the middle of cornfields
To flourish
On the windswept prairies
Where the buffalo
And nomadic Dakota once roamed
Until my tribe moved in
With its plows and oxen
Its silos and corncribs
To break the raw prairie sod
To erect this improbable monolith
I am sweating in reverie
Amid a fresh onslaught of steam

5:38

Strong medicine of the steam
Sear and hiss of steam
Almost a serum to breathe
A scythe inside the chest
Heads draped ghostly under towels
Dizzy with the heat
Some gasping for breath
Some fleeing our sweat lodge
The future of my tribe in doubt
The price of our healing work is high
The costs take their toll
My people tired yet well-fed
My people rich yet stressed
My people weary of meetings
My people living in perpetual fear
Of productivity reports
Medicare forms

Endless documentation
Wrath and scrutiny
Of insurance companies
The great ongoing morass
Of health care reform
Everyone his own shaman
Seeking his vision here in the stream
Every idea big or small
Evaluated by a system of sub-tribes
One committee merging into another
In order to help our tribe
Stay solvent
As council by council we chant
We chant our scared mission
The needs of the patient come first
Even as we sacrifice
Even as we sweat and drip
Toward temporary release
The saving remnant of a vision
That may never arrive
In the rank heat of our steam

5:39
Who is our sacred fire-
Keeper no one's ever seen
Year by year more
Mysterious beyond his wall
Guardian of my tribe's sacred texts
My tribe's earliest pictographs
Scrawled on limestone
Quarried from an ancient
Shallow semitropical seabed
Some believe he's a spirit
Risen from the dead
That if you had a key
You'd find no bones
Just an empty tomb
I imagine a woodshed
At one end of his spacious
Utility closet
From the other the gush
Of a giant spring
I among my tribesmen

All of us sweating for a vision
Amid the bliss
And agony of the steam
Delirious in the steam
Solemn in the steam
Back to the Dream Time
Survey markers still fresh
Hatchet marks fresh
In section-corner oak saplings
Land with the dew still on it
A Peaceable Kingdom
Virgin sod black as the coal
A prairie wildflower garden
Through which the founder of our tribe
Sailed by Conestoga wagon
Arriving here as an inspector
Of copper mines
River ferry pilot
Yeoman farmer
Part-time doctor sometimes
Treating a sick horse
Until a war-time summons
Enchanted drumbeat
From the Supreme Chief
In distant Washington
Abraham Lincoln

5:41
Now the Great Uprising
Now the slaughter of innocents
Our women and children forced to flee
To hide for days in cattail sloughs
Raped and scalped
Our women to take up pitchforks
To tuck their hair in and pose
Like men going into battle
The founder of my tribe
Treating the freshly wounded
The Little Doctor
Barking swift orders
In a saloon surrounded by siege
Deep in this land that was not quite our land
From sea to shining sea

Until our Council of Chiefs
In the capitol of St. Paul
By order of our mightiest fort
The White House
In far-off Washington
Sent troops
To quell and vanquish
To expel and banish
To secure our borders
To separate friend from foe
To harass and punish
To chase and skirmish
To root out and arrest
These enemy combatants
One nation
Under the Great Spirit
Indivisible
With mass execution for all

5:43

Shakopee and Big Eagle hanged
Mankato bludgeoned by cannonball
Little Crow shot in the back raspberry-picking
Red Cloud deported to rot on his reservation
Crazy Horse bayoneted in the kidney
Sitting Bull turned into a cartoon character
Chief Seattle chased to exhaustion
The last cut down in the snows
Last of the Ghost Dancers
Starving, mad, hysterical
Cut down by Gatling gun
With Chief Big Foot
Limbs askew in the bloodsmeared
Snow at Wounded Knee

5:44

In the steam the hooves
Of history paw and tamp the earth
In the stream a trader's
Mouth stuffed with ants and grass
In the steam settler children
Each with a pitchfork

Thrust through the forelock
In the steam the scream
Of arrow wounds
Flushed with whiskey
In the steam wriggling papooses
Bayoneted in the temple
A stained beard dripping
Tobacco juice, big dumb
Laugh Nits make lice
In the steam a thousand ponies
Swoop down in a pageantry
Of face paint and eagle feathers
Thunder and dust
In the steam a vast white garment
Stretched across the prairies
Of southern Minnesota
Saturates with blood

5:46

In the steam 38 Dakota sing from nooses
Blindfolded they sing
(Can you hear them sing?)
Draft horses spurred then whipped
The platform rips away
Feet kicking until they jerk
Wildly then dangle
To a listless halt
In cloak and tunic
The doctors arrive by lanternlight
To haggle over cadavers
One called Cut Nose
His carcass dismembered
Tossed down an outhouse hole
Retrieved from the dung
By the founder of my tribe
The short-statured horse-and-buggy
Doctor who started all this
Whose unborn sons would lead us
Whose sons would become surgeon
Whose sons would become shaman
Whose sons would become legend
Whose sons would learn anatomy
From a kettle of bones

Articulating the skeleton
That hung in our Founding Father's study
The archived scalp and tanned skin of this
Hanged Red Man an impossible
Conundrum and perpetual gift
For the advancement of modern medicine
From the greatest of our Great White Fathers
In far-off Washington
Whose pocked and craggy face
Stares forever east from Paha Sapa
Across Great Plains
Over Killdeer Mountain
Over Whitestone Hill
Toward Birch Coulee
Toward New Ulm
Toward Fort Ridgley
Toward Wood Lake
Toward Montevideo
Toward Camp Release
Toward Mankato
Toward Fort Snelling
Toward Rochester
Dynamited into the side of a mountain
Staring forever in the direction of my tribe
Staring as so few can into his own heart
Into my tribe's heart
And out into the fallen world
At the same time
Staring until the end of human time

5:51

I am in reverie here in the steam
Over my tribe's origins in the steam
Naked among my gifted and talented
My world-renowned tribe of healers
Who devote long hours
Overtime without pay
Who labor in spare time writing papers
Who rise without complaint
All hours of sleepless nights
To beeping pagers
Who give their whole lives over
Who give their personal cell numbers over
I am in awe and reverie here in the steam
My tribe of healers soaking
Away their cares in the steam
Where out of good manners
And Midwestern reserve
And Minnesota Nice no one speaks
Where one rarely speaks in the sacred
Moments of purifying oneself
In the never-ending surcease of the steam

5:53

Ah, yes, our antiseptic-scented steam
Same as the steam of the ancients
Chanting words from a different time
Naked in the steam of thermal creeks
Our steam the same as their steam
As steam rising from fumaroles
Across the geyser basins of Yellowstone
Steam no different than Rocky Mountain steam
Sacred stream rising from the great mineral
Hot springs of Thermopolis, Wyoming
Steam of purest boiling spring water
Yes, the journey of my tribe of healers
Begins and ends just west of the Mississippi
Where my tribe has everything it needs
Here in the bluff valleys of the Zumbro
One fine morning my tribe will awake
One day here in the stream inside our cramped
Sweat lodge inside the men's locker room
Of the Dan Abraham Healthy Living Center
One day my tribe will leave this world
And dream itself back to reality

Neale Torgrimson
They Are Coming Up Your Street

heard this story secondhand. In Minneapolis, hell, the world, in the days after George Floyd's death that's about as good as seeing it with your own eyeballs and, let's face it, you only got two of those. Not that you could trust those either.

A friend of a friend and his partner drove up to the protests around the 3rd Precinct. It's the second night of protesting, the Wednesday after George Floyd's death on the Memorial Day Monday. Sometime before dusk, he parks a ways from the 3rd. There were protests at the 3rd the night before, more confrontational than anything else around town. Folks are already starting to flee the action on Lake Street as even more people are filing in. The first person he and his partner see is a shirtless man speedwalking with a stack of brake pads cradled in his arms.

"AutoZone's wide open for the taking," the stranger said as he passed by, "You can take whatever you want."

"How'd you know where to look?" this friend of a friend asked.

"I used the computer," said the shirtless man as he turned his back on the smoke and the rancor and the setting sun.

I used the computer.

This man went to the AutoZone, past the police riot, around the hundreds of protestors, ignoring the plumes of tear gas, the hail of rubber bullets, the salvos of marker rounds that preceded those, stepped through the shattered front window, went up to the front desk, booted up the computers, navigated the proprietary search engine for his make and model of the brake pads he needed, found his bearings in their rows of ransacked shelving in a building full of chemicals, rubber tires, and synthetic oil that at this point might already be burning, grabbed all the brake pads he could carry, and booked it down Lake.

Little has made sense before or after those days. It feels daunting to try and overlay some sensible chronology over the past few months. There's time before the pandemic, there's time before George Floyd's death, and the splintered wreckage of time after. I am writing this at the end of the summer, a season of tumult in a year of tumult. It all feels like yesterday and, somehow, it feels as if it hasn't even happened yet. Time warps itself around the black hole gravity of each event according to some sort of cosmic accounting that probably makes sense in the end, but who has the mind for that? It all feels ... felt ... feels almost quantum. In those days it was as if you were experiencing the events beyond the scope of your surroundings. Experiencing what was in front of you right in the now, what was happening across town, what was happening across the world, what you were hearing on the news, and what you were hearing on social media all at once.

During the days of the protests and most definitely in the days after, there were many attempts at narrative control. We're all trying to process this moment in alignment with our experiences, our ideologies, and affirm the choices we've always made. No one viewpoint could ever encompass all of this mess. It's like looking upon the jagged coast of some unknown continent and knowing what's just beyond the horizon is unrecognizable with the land before you.

The best one can hope to do is to center the narrative around their own experiences, but to understand that those experiences are themselves de-centered and in no way a proxy for others.

When I heard that George Floyd had been murdered, I experienced a sort of deja vu. I remember driving by Cup Foods a few years past and listening to the radio as the verdict of the Philando Castile murder was breaking. Officer Yanez, who shot Philando in front of his partner and infant child, was to be acquitted. I sat at a red light at 38th and Chicago, the same intersection where George Floyd would be murdered a few years later and wondered if the people knew. It was threatening to rain, but there were still people on the street walking about and going along with their lives. Part of me thought that, deep down, they already knew and that only I had to be told.

Errands then took me to the Target across Lake from the 3rd Precinct, where I saw a young black clerk stocking the shelves. It was the "As Seen on TV" aisle. You know, the one crammed with five-finger oven mitts, modular onion choppers, extra wicking dish rags, and shirts for dogs of all sizes. As he was stocking the shelves, I thought to myself, "How can he do it? How can he stand here and stock all this stupid plastic shit for meager pay when our government, our society would justify his murder by the hands of an agent of the state?"

The simple answer is he couldn't. How could he? Sooner, later, you break. I retraced my steps that Wednesday morning after George Floyd's death, driving past Target towards 38th and Chicago. The road was littered with rocks from the berm of the parking lot, broken glass, an iron plate used as a makeshift barrier, plastic parts from tear gas canisters jettisoned after impact, and empty milk jugs, more than I could count. It was maybe the first round of fake news. Someone said that milk helped to flush out tear gas from the eyes and sinuses. Supposedly this is true for Pepper Spray, but with Tear Gas it helps to trap the irritants in and regular old water is better. Volunteers would douse the reeling protestors with jugs of the stuff and they'd walk away still in anguish, their faces literally white with pain.

Activists have long been vocal about the tensions with police. There was Jamar Clark in 2015, Philando Castile in 2016, Justine Damond in 2017, and others, all contributed to a bone-deep community distrust with the police. They talked of prior instances where things seemed as if they were going to boil over, but for the intervention of community and movement leaders. They were able to stop it before, but there was no stopping it now. Foresight is one thing and sight is another. Not even the sharpest of mind's eye could have anticipated the speed and expansiveness of how it could all fall apart, nor the feeling of seeing it all go up in smoke.

Driving from Target to Cup, I tried to retrace how I felt on the day that Yanez got acquitted, foolishly thinking that what I was about to experience was going to be similar. I live in the Seward neighborhood of Minneapolis, a mile or so north of the 3rd Precinct. From Wednesday onward I woke up with a sore throat wondering if it was the start of Covid symptoms or, as was the case, from breathing in burning buildings. I would walk down to Lake in the mornings before work and take inventory of the devastation: what smoldered and what was spared.

The destruction on Lake was immeasurable. There are people who will tell you that they are just buildings and they can be rebuilt. Perhaps, they are right. There are numbers and figures totaling the number of arsons or estimating the overall damage. Perhaps they are accurate. The psychic damage, however, the pain and the trauma and the hopelessness, was beyond perception, like staring down into a canyon that not even daylight could reach the depths of. Numbers and words were insufficient in that moment and they fail us still.

I was worried that the police were going to make the 3rd their Alamo and hold the fort at all costs. If they did, they would have still lost the Precinct, but with many fatalities, or maybe they would have held it and pushed the mayhem outward into the unburnt residential neighborhoods. It was with that fear that I decided to get out of town and spend the weekend on my parent's farm in Southeast Minnesota. It was a privilege, but one I felt I needed to take advantage of.

It is important to note that I was not born in Minnesota, but overseas. My parents worked in refugee resettlement and from them I would hear the tales of escape that their clients had. Most of the refugees they worked with came from

Vietnam, Cambodia, and Laos and, even though they fled different countries, stories of their flight were remarkably similar. "They are coming up your street. Pack your bags and go. You have ten minutes or less." Who they were and why they were coming was always different, coded in the particular context of whatever tumult they were fleeing from.

As I was packing up my bags, I got a text from a neighbor. "Someone just said they are coming up your street." The cops had begun indiscriminately tear gassing and firing rubber bullets at people, pushing the protests up the road. I immediately thought of the refugees. "They are coming up your street. Pack your bags and go. You have ten minutes or less."

The next few days on the farm were surreal, spent in a sort of pastoral serenity interspersed with manic calls to see if friends were okay and frightening searches for what remained. Still, I was safe.

When we returned a few days later things had calmed down slightly. By calm I mean the Governor had mandated a curfew and called in the National Guard to enforce it. By calm I mean that my neighbors and myself were filling buckets of water to put out potential fires. By calm I mean the community formed patrols to keep a watch. By calm I mean that incendiary devices were discovered through town, including one found in the bushes two houses from mine. By calm I mean that armed far right extremists were cruising around the neighborhoods.

So, maybe calm wasn't the right word, but after the 3rd Precinct was overtaken, things at least seemed to spread out, to dilute a bit. Black Lives Matter protests started to happen in other cities and states in solidarity with the protests in Minneapolis. It was encouraging to see how the protests had touched a chord, even overseas. One of the most startling things I saw during the uprising, online or off, was a picture of 38th and Chicago on the front page of Das Bild, the German language newspaper. For a moment, Minnesota was the center of the world.

Officials eventually lifted the curfew. Leadership began to retake control and the worst elements of the unrest went home or went somewhere else. The City Council pledged to "defund the police," a concept whose meaning and technical legality is being argued about to this day. A temporary homeless shelter at the Minneapolis Sheraton was followed by a massive, 500+ encampment in Powderhorn Park. The shelters allowed social workers to help manage the homeless community, but each shelter became overwhelmed by sex trafficking, drug use, and violence. The city, and some advocates in the community, deemed the situation untenable and the encampment was spread out across the vast park system. Violent crime is up over the summer, a phenomenon that happened in Baltimore the months after the Freddie Gray riots ended and many sociologists predicted would happen here. The areas around Powderhorn Park, Downtown, and on the city's North side seem to be affected the most.

There is difficulty in finding an ending to this in part because it hasn't ended. The main fire has gone out, but the coals are still quite hot. There is a hope and bond within the community that has not been felt before, but there is exhaustion too and a fear that the right moves done in the wrong way will undo everything. In the days after George Floyd's death, there was a clear and universal feeling that nothing would ever be the same, that yesterday, whatever day that was, was history, never to be seen or felt again. Today, at the end of summer, a season of tumult in a year of tumult, where every day felt like it was threatening to storm, I feel the same.

Wm. Anthony Connolly

Saint Albino Thomas: A Murder

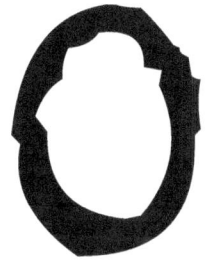

ne for sorrow

The work of soul alchemy begins with a black crow. The midnight-black bird symbolizes the initial flight of an alchemist alighting into inner space the while the sensual world subsides. Alchemical texts call this juncture the blackening, the *nigredo* experience, a putrefaction, decomposition—death. By the penetration of the inner soul, where burns an interior fire the matter of corporality starts to putrefy, to its primal matter. This process is also called *cooking*. The black vestiges are closed up in a vessel or flask, and heated. Thus through the trope of the black crow we have the stepping out in consciousness from the world of the physical senses away from the restrictions that bind us to the physical body. The alchemist takes wing.

Two for joy

Whenever I eat processed cheese sandwiches, a modern product of culinary alchemy, I think of crows. And when I remember crows, or think about them long enough, I recall a certain time, the very early nineteen seventies, and I recall a childhood albino name Thom; he made the angry crow fly away.

It was the fall when I was six that I entered the second grade, only to be told, about a week later, that I would instead be enrolled in the first grade. My family and I had recently moved and the grade configuration or alignment was uncertain science at best. If I'd stayed in the second grade many things would today be different. But I was dropped back, not in a cognitive developmental kind of way, you understand, but simply out of a wont to do what was best for my progression. I wasn't in the decision-making process, to be honest.

It was in the first grade I met Thom J. He was an albino—white hair, eyebrows, eyelashes and the palest skin I'd ever seen in my six years of world-traveling. I was meant to meet Thom and for the rest of my years I have Thom to thank for many things. For my progression and some of my joy. I have never forgotten Thom, and here's why.

He made the crow go away.

Three for a girl

If Thom wasn't strictly a textbook albino, he was close so I take it back: I don't think his eyelashes were white, they might have been black. Thom wore glasses. Silver wire frames. He ate cheese sandwiches every day for lunch—processed cheese slices between white Wonder Bread and walked with his shoulder in a permanent shrug. We ate lunch together with Yvette, a redheaded girl we both admired, mostly for her red hair. She also gave us three sparkling indigo sequins to hold in our palms and told us they were magic—they of course were not, it dawned on me much later.

Going to this school, that fall, the colors of red, orange and dark brown filtered with bright autumnal light comes to mind, there was darkness too. The walk was about two blocks from our house to the elementary school—Fort la Reine; the school was on Thirteenth Street and we lived on Fifteenth Street.

It's a squat school, with a large front playing field skirting the town's main street. But mostly, the school was nestled in a forest canopy of tree limbs, and shaded streets. The trip from the house to the school took five minutes, tops; longer for children easily distracted or otherwise, but generally a quick and safe journey.

But for that fall, the trip was a perilous one the first few weeks of school in early September. Children were being attacked by a swooping crow. The crow would swoop down on children, beak flicking strands of hair, pecking at wool caps; wings swooshing by shoulders and headwear. Children walked with their lunch pails up on their heads. The fear was always that the large black bird would pluck out your eyes. I saw it myself, the bird, diving from the tree limbs to the throng of students walking to school. I saw the scattering crowd as the crow sorties menaced the students. It wasn't an old wives' tale told to get students to walk directly to school or home without doddering. I saw it swoop out of the sky and fly, like a daredevil at my school mates. I ran with my orange plastic lunch pail atop my head. I ran. I didn't want my own eyes plucked out of my head.

The crow turned up in many classroom discussions, but the black menace disappeared after one particular item in Show-And-Tell. It was Albino Thom. Thom J. Processed cheese-slice eater. It disappeared when Thom showed us what to do.

Four for a boy

It was a very large scroll.

It looked like a large, old archaeological map when he carried it in his arms, tucked against his body, carried like a rifle. It was crinkled and frayed. It made a rustling, crinkly, noise when he unrolled it at the front of the class, using a number of student desks moved together to prop it up for us to see. Its white surface, once unrolled, was covered with color, in a long assemblage of characters and apparitions. It was Thom's mind.

Whenever he had a bad dream, Thom would arise the next morning and with colored pencils and crayons he would proceed to draw the monster onto the page, the continuous scroll that he rolled back up once he'd captured the creature onto the parchment, captured forever.

He said whenever he put the bad thing down on

paper, it never came back. It was as good as a four-leaf clover, a rabbit's foot or one of those silver dollar coins from a vending machine.

That day, the last creature on the scroll, the still unfinished scroll, was a large black crow in horrifyingly mid-flight.

Five for silver

Thom and I would go our separate ways after elementary school, largely on account of where our parents lived, we were assigned different schools. Fortunately, in high school, and there being only two in my hometown, we were reunited. It was good to see him again, and we became acquaintances, but not what could be characterized as chums or best pals. Thom had retained much of the shyness and quirkiness he'd displayed in elementary school, he still walked as if he was in permanent shrug. His eyes twitched. We went through high school together, graduated in the same class and I heard he attended a liberal arts school in the one of the Dakotas. He was a drummer and the school would allow him to develop his musical skills as well as other academic pursuits.

One summer I returned home, this would be a few years after high school, and ran into some old friends, mutual friends of mine and Thom's, and I asked of his whereabouts.

"He's not well," said Robert T, a good friend of Thom's. "He's on medication. He might be schizophrenic."

My mind went instantly back to his scroll. How he dispensed with his monsters by capturing them on paper. I wondered if he'd stopped doing the little exercise when he reached the end, the end of his scroll. I told Robert about Thom's scroll and he looked at me as if I'd been telling him a fairy tale. This is a common reaction. I often speak of things I've been thinking, but not said aloud and when I do say them out loud—*in media res*—people are understandably baffled or confused. I'm either over-enthusiastic or mumble under my uncertainty. Suddenly, partially, recalling an old rhyme. Of course, I had pictured in my mind Thom's crows and had been hearing the old nursery rhyme, with crows in my head, and for the life of me then, even when I asked a perplexed Robert to help me, I could not complete the rhyme. We stopped at "five crows for silver …"

Six for gold

It stays with you, what you learn from the people you come to meet and know in your lifetime. We eat each other's pain or feel the vibration of another's golden joy years later, each little thing a gift, each a gospel. Saint Albino Thom. The gospel of Thom was a scroll, and the idea that scares us can be tamed through record.

I hope he is not still sick. I hope that he is well today and can live without the torture of his mental condition. I write this down, the only way I know how, to chase away the murder of crows over Thom.

Seven for a secret never to be told.

I was told when you hear a crow's caw, thank the Creator for them and ask yourself if you're walking the right path in life. Crows are reminders to live an honest, healthy, positive life. Back in the fall of those nineteen seventies, the days of dim skies, and death from above it was Thom, and only Thom I told the secret I was not to reveal: I had been molested by a male babysitter. I hadn't told a soul. I thought I had done something bad. I asked him to do his scroll thing. It was as if I asked him to swallow darkness for me.

He just nodded, peering at me through his silver-rimmed glasses, his brilliant albino visage seeming—to me now years later—as a brightness flickering from within. He had not heard a word I'd said, because I hadn't said them aloud. I wanted to, but I couldn't. I said instead something about sequins being magical. I was just a kid, who believed the world was full of magic, but who also discovered it was one of danger. I swallowed the desire to speak of it down with my lunch. We finished our cheese sandwiches in silence and stared, as we often did, at wondrous Yvette. Three sweaty sequins lined the palm of my hand.

I've thought of Thom off and on throughout the years and wondered too if I had told him, might I have turned out differently? Less tortured and ashamed. If I'd been a better friend to him, would he have told me about his incessant monsters?

I write this down knowing the crow is still out there, in the air, circling. I write this down. I write this down.

SHIPWRECKT BOOKS

New Releases
Summer 2020

www.shipwrecktbooks.press

Lee Henschel Jr.

R

he Ojibway word for not being sure of something is *endogwen*. Throughout the fourteenth century the pandemic called Black Death, or the Bubonic plague, killed an estimated seventy-five to two hundred million people. Doesn't really matter today, though, because just recently our state finalized an agreement to buy storage facilities for human remains, while at the same time our governor announced plans for the phased reopening of our economy. A conundrum that resonates with conditions during the Black Death, because the information on COVID-19 is contradictory, inaccurate, incorrect or misleading, and always subject to change. To be this uncertain is to revisit the dark ages.

Even so, people believe that uncertain times are the catalyst for change. So what? At one point during the Black Death authorities in London went so far as to prohibit all public gatherings, including performances at the Globe Theater. As a result, Shakespeare had no place to put on his plays, so he made use of his gift by creating a new sonnet form. Very nice, but I'm sure the unwashed masses questioned how this new Shakespearean sonnet could have any relevance for the people who had already died from the Black Death.

In the United States, as of late May of 2020, there are about 71,000 people who have already died from COVID-19. Some of the dead have no names. They were probably living on the street and are now buried in mass graves. The exact number is *endogwen*. Meanwhile, the fiscal pundits and politicians remind us that they're uncertain, as well, and that only time will tell.

Yes, the answers will come in time. But not all of them. And some will remain cloaked forever. Except it's not the answers that determine who we are at this moment. Instead, it is the nature of our questions. For they are the measure of who we are and what we are thinking. Who'll be the next in line? Does COVID-19 possess some kind of evil self-awareness? And the people we love, how many of them will lie among the dead? Is the virus some sort of biological weapon brewed in a laboratory and unleashed upon the world? And what about our money? Our smart phone signal. Or the mortgage. Will the liquor stores and gun shops remain open?

There is a satire. *Candide*. Written by Voltaire in 1759. Toward the end Candide claims that after all the horror, after all the misfortune, there's really only one thing we can do. Tend our own garden.

But what is the essence of our own garden? Since the onslaught of COVID-19 the essence of my own garden has transformed. Because in my own garden there now walks a homeless man. R. I met R a few years back while I was riding my bike and he was walking at the lake. Didn't actually meet him, though, because for an entire year I'd just say hello to him, and then ride on.

R displays only a few traits of the homeless. He carries a lot of baggage, to be sure. And he's always alone, minding his own business. Quiet. Almost invisible. He drew my attention, though, because of his footwear, and his clothes. Warm, sturdy boots in winter. Pretty good tennis shoes in the spring, summer and fall. Clean clothes. Never worn thin or ragged. And he's not ragged, either He's clean. Clean shaven. With healthy, if weathered Caucasian skin. Bald as a monk.

All in all, something about R seemed out of place. But it wasn't any of my business. So I always said hi, if only to acknowledge his existence. Then, at first light on the Sunday of Memorial Day weekend three years ago, I saw R sitting alone in the pavilion by the lake. A cool, wet, morning. Nothing stirring. Just R and me. A good moment to actually stop and say more than just hello. I told him my name, and he told me his. But R is a man who keeps a low profile, so I won't say his name. Only R.

"Did you stay dry last night?" I asked.

"Yes."

"Do you sleep outside in the winter, too?"

"Yes."

"You could fall asleep and freeze to death."

"No, my feet get cold and they wake me up."

"The snack bar's open soon. Can I buy you breakfast?"

"No, thank you, I have food."

"A cup of coffee then?"

"No, I don't drink coffee."

"Well, nice meeting you R. I'll say hi next time I see you."

And I always do say hi. And since then I've learned something more about R. Once, a year ago, I saw him with a bunch of pens and pencils, and he was writing in a note pad. I told him I was a writer, too. I asked him what he liked to write.

"Astrology."

"Do you have a pencil sharpener?"

"No."

"Would it be okay if I gave you one?"

"Okay."

After that I carried a small sharpener with me for the next time I saw him.

Because of his clean clothes and his general good health, I wondered if R was really homeless. And if he was a writer, then maybe he was writing some sort of homeless story. Something like *Black Like Me*, by John Howard Griffin. But it would be *Homeless Like Me*, by R.

Once I asked him if he still had the pencil sharpener.

"No. I lost it."

So I don't think R is actually a writer, because homeless or not, a writer does not lose his pencil sharpener. Well, at least I wouldn't.

It doesn't really matter, though, if R's a writer or not, because there's still something about him. Some unknown quality. And it is this . . . once, after I'd earned a slight measure of his trust, he risked showing me something of his own. His drawings. It turns out R is a talented portrait artist. Some are real people, easily recognized. Some are unknown, perhaps unknowable. All of them drawn with pencil on cheap paper and tucked in a folder he always carries.

Once I asked him if he ever drew sailing ships. Frigates from the Golden Age of Sail, for instance.

"No."

"Well, if you ever draw one, I'd like to see it. I might buy it."

He makes a face. "I don't draw for money."

Last week I saw him again in the pavilion and stopped in to say hi. He showed me more of his drawings.

"Have you drawn all your life?"

"I quit after high school. That was . . . forty-four years ago. Then I took it up again a few years ago."

"Was it hard to get it back?"

"No. It's instinct."

"Do you remember when I asked if you ever draw sailing ships?"

"Yes. But I only draw what inspires me."

"Well, if you're ever inspired to draw a frigate, I'd like to put it on the cover of my next book."

This time he doesn't make a face. Instead, he gives me a vague smile. Does this mean that maybe someday he'll draw me a fine frigate? I'm not sure. It remains *endogwen*.

What I do know is that R's homeless and vulnerable. Hopefully never to become just another COVID-19 statistic, but instead will live for a long time, and drawing what inspires him.

Rob Hardy
Two Variations

Grounded

Is our world gone? We say "Farewell."
Is a new world coming? We welcome it.
—Lyndon B. Johnson (quoted on pages 20-21
of the U.S. passport)

My new passport has never been anywhere.
It lies in an old shoebox,
like a dead pet awaiting burial,
with unspent euros and European plug
adaptors,
maps of Athens and central London
and other places we visited in a different world.
The box says New Balance.
Sometimes I take out my expired passport
and look at the stamps—
London, Frankfurt, Osaka, Athens—
remembering how I stood in line
to receive them like a sacrament,
remembering the places themselves, the pieces
of myself left there, irretrievable.
The future feels like unclaimed baggage.
There's nowhere else in the world I can go.
I'm thinking of getting a better box.

Covid-19 Variations

Corvid: a type of bird, crow or raven,
an absence of light perched
ominously on the bare branch
of a roadside tree,
descending after the impact
to dance.

Ovid: a poet who wrote *We are slow*
to believe in the things that cause us harm
and Abundance has made me poor.

Comorbid: existing simultaneously
in a patient. As in, anxiety and depression
are frequently comorbid. As in all
the comorbidities of March:
sap running and ice going out,
the song of the red-winged blackbird
and the color brown,
chapped hands and empty shelves.

Covid-19: at this distance from yesterday
and one another, sometimes
we have to be the bird
singing somewhere in the woods, who for now
exists only as its song.

Saturday, March 14, 2020

Raymond Luczak
The Crow Lady

he Paul Bunyan statuette had been carved from wood with paint fleshing out its features: a blue cap, a thick black beard, a red shirt and black suspenders, denim blue pants, brown boots, and an ax resting on its shoulder. It stayed on the TV in front of the rabbit-eared antenna. It stood twelve inches tall, watching the shadow, reeking of whiskey and cigarettes, putting his hand on her mouth as he demanded his way on the sofa.

As she tried to scissor him off by closing her thighs and biting at the sweaty fingers, she caught sight of the statuette. Splayed against her will, she stared at its cheerful face caught in a ray of afternoon sunlight from a window near the TV. Later she would swear she saw a single tear trickle down its cheek. She was twelve years old, and the year was 1989.

*

The morning after Olivia walked through the living room. The maroon sofa looked the same as before. The statuette hadn't moved from the TV. There was no evidence—not even blood—of what had happened the night before. Had she dreamed such violence? But hadn't she cleaned herself of the blood the night before?

The statuette looked different, but just *what* had changed? It had been in the family for three generations here in Minnesota. It was initially unpainted and unvarnished, but her great grandfather brought it to an artist who painted it to look like the giant lumberjack. When the paint began to chip, her grandfather had it repainted and varnished. It stood in her grandfather's house until he died, so Dad took it for himself. It was his favorite toy growing up. He was still bitter about having to sell his parents' farm where he'd grown up and moving to Albert Lea where he mowed park lawns and drove a snowplow for the city. They lived on the edge between town and country.

She looked up at the statuette and recalled how Dad had told stories before Mom died. "Here's another funny bit my pa used to tell me. He said, 'People got real confused when it felt like night at noon. All they had to do was to look up and there he was! They were all standing in his shadow. Paul only wanted to know when lunch would be ready.

"'Sometimes there was no stopping him. Everyone had to be real careful at night when Paul lay down to sleep because his butt would be so high like the hills. If a bird landed on his butt, he could let out a huge fart that lit up the sky. The smell was worse than skunk and lasted for a week. That's why nobody ever served him tubfuls of beans.' Pa chortled. 'You know how big Lake Superior is, right? Scuba divers swear they've found the exact spot where Paul used to take his baths, right near Duluth. They went down there in the water and found two big flat holes right next to each other. They figured that had to be where he must've sat, right? Makes me wonder what would happen if he farted underwater. I bet the water just …' He made a poof sound and gestured with his hands. '… all over Duluth. Everyone would get so wet it'd take them two days to dry." Pa burst out laughing.

Mom said, "Oh, that's so gross! I hate it when you tell those stories." But there was a sparkle in her eye.

Olivia came closer to the statuette, only to be interrupted.

"Hey, we gotta get going." It was the shadow's voice. Her father. Dad.

*

At school she felt the numbing pain down there and dragged her feet up and down the steps. When she sat in the classroom, the sound of boys laughing in the back of the room took on a sinister overtone. They hadn't changed, but she had. She couldn't look directly at any boy, and she felt a twinge of nausea when she looked at her male teachers. Could they all be like him behind closed doors? Why would any girl want a boyfriend? That *thing* was—she didn't want to remember its size and brunt-ness. She was a new person now, only that she had no words to describe what she was feeling.

She hadn't known either what to feel when she watched Mom wither from a thick-haired woman with a full figure into a bald ghost with stick arms, trying her wan best to smile each time anyone entered her room. Even the double mastectomies couldn't save her. Even though Olivia was only eleven years old, she was already feeling the blush of puberty. She wanted to ask Mom so many questions, but she didn't want to seem selfish. It was disconcerting whenever acquaintances commented on what a brave woman her mother was on top of pointing out her startling physical resemblance to Mom.

Nine months after Mom died, Dad woke up one morning on the sofa after having come home drunk the night before, he blinked his eyes and gazed at Olivia. "Damn," he said. "I don't know why I didn't see it before." He wiped his mouth. "You look exactly like Lois when I first saw her."

*

Once violated, all she wanted was to die. She didn't care how. She didn't want the residue of diesel from his fingers, the hovering stink of his sweat, the disgusting saliva from his mouth. She imagined death as a safe place where no one could touch her body. She knew in her bones that he would never be allowed up in the heavens. Condemned to the pits of hell, he would feel the nonstop singe of fire burning his thick eyebrows. His body would never burn completely, and the barbed wire wrapped around his chest would sear his skin. Every time he moved he fell onto a plateau of stone that seemed cool at first but within seconds would turn hot as the coils of a stovetop. It didn't matter where he moved; his naked feet would feel the sigh of coolness only to stumble onto sizzle.

Floating, she would feel whole in a cloudless sky. Her hearing would be so precise that she could hear any man's first utterance of untoward desire for little girls where she would swoop down and knock such men about to have their way so these girls would never be touched. She would knock the men with such force that their heads would fall against a sharp object and hemorrhage so much blood that these girls could simply escape.

*

Olivia, now a sophomore, hadn't paid much attention to Mitchell at first. He stood alone in the doorway between the stairs and the long wall of lockers on the second floor. Quite short for his age, he wore black glasses, a polo shirt, and khaki pants. His blond hair was slicked back with gel. He hesitated with every movement he made, but when she saw the afternoon sunlight behind him, she had a flashback of the statuette. He was that still. Then, out of nowhere, a gaggle of varsity football players climbed up the stairs and pushed Mitchell aside. His glasses fell off, and she winced at the sound of sneakers stomping on them. The footballers looked down at the shattered glasses and laughed. They walked past her as if it was just another day for them.

She glanced back at Mitchell. His face remained wooden.

After lunch, they fell into standing next to each other, rarely talking, by the lockers waiting for their afternoon classes to start. She was afraid of the sound of her own voice, and more afraid of the sound of his voice, which sounded nothing like the voices of boys and men she knew. It was light and airy. Sometimes they rolled their eyes at each other after hearing a trio of girls giggling, but they hadn't yet learned to speak the common language of misfits.

*

Though her body showed no bruises, she ached

all over. Any pressure of touch, no matter how tender, caused pain to ripple throughout her body. The straps of her bra nearly made her cry, but she knew she couldn't go braless. Everyone would snicker, and then the principal would summon her to his office and demand that she go home and wear something suitable. And what would Dad say? Sitting at her desk was agony.

By noon she felt herself on the verge of tears. She couldn't look directly at anyone. Standing in line at the cafeteria, she maintained a short distance from everyone out of fear of being accidentally touched. Then she heard her math teacher, Mr. Finnstrom, laughing as he ambled toward the food. His self-congratulatory laughs always reminded her of Dad. Then she heard a yelp. She turned and saw that by the entrance three football players were calling Mitchell names: "Queer. Faggot. Pussyboy." When one of them began to shove Mitchell against the doorframe, she felt nausea take hold inside her. She had experienced it each time the shadow forced her down against the sofa, the wall, whatever happened to be there to block her from running away; it was the sensation of vomit pushing upward at the base of her throat, her armpits breaking into puddles of sweat, she needed to die, *like right now*—she grabbed a pair of butter knives and tried to stab herself in the stomach. She didn't hear the sudden hush of silence punctuated by gasps as she crashed into oblivion on the floor.

She woke up in a hospital room. She found herself slightly bound to the mattress; she couldn't move. Someone had strapped her arms to the bed railing. She wasn't wearing her own clothes; just a simple gown with tiny flowers printed on them. She felt chilly. The synthetic blanket atop of her wasn't enough to keep her warm. *Water*, she kept thinking.

"I need water," she shouted. Her parched tongue made her sound mangled.

Amidst the soft rustle outside her door, she heard the shadow's voice, full of concern, echoing from the hallway. She closed her eyes and commanded the bile not to rise up inside her.

She would smile and perfect her lies. She would get through this. Only two more years.

*

During her week-long stay at the Treesburg Institute, Olivia felt like a helium balloon tethered to the floor where the little people underneath her pulled her along like the massive cartoon characters floating in Macy's Thanksgiving Day Parade. She couldn't tell anyone about Dad, so she made the grieving for Mom her excuse. She hadn't known how much she missed Mom until she bawled out details about her during group therapy, and again to Dr. Ellis, a psychiatrist with round glasses and graying hair.

Otherwise she sat in front of a panoramic window that overlooked a well-kept yard half-circled by naked trees; the first snow hadn't yet arrived. On the second day she made a spectacular discovery by the window. Rain was falling rather heavily, and yet on a thick branch off a tree near her right, a large crow stood and kept its wings tucked in. It did not move, but its eyes were fixated on her. When she got up for the restroom, its eyes followed her. *Could it really see me?* When she returned, the crow hopped a bit closer to the window. She took a chair closer to the window, and there for an hour they simply observed each other. When the rain stopped, it took flight.

Every day she sat by the window. It didn't matter what kind of weather it was, but her crow was always there. She began to wonder about the lives of crows. What gave them their strength? She began to dream of having wings so black that she could vanish into the night the second the shadow touched her.

*

Olivia came to dread coming home after her twice-a-week sessions with Dr. Ellis. Dad would be waiting in the living room, right on the same sofa where he had turned into shadow, and with only one question: "Did you tell her about us?"

She shook her head no.

"You can't tell. *Ever.*"

"No, I won't." She climbed the stairs and closed the door. She would lose herself in the intricacies of homework. She knew he was always watching her from the darkness of hallway, waiting for the moment when she was done. She could hear him trying to sip his whiskey quietly and lighting another cigarette.

Before the shadow first began to consume her, she always did much of her homework on the bus so she could have more free time. Not anymore. She dragged her minutes over each geometry problem, the dull textbook descriptions of world history, and the ponderous essays she wrote and rewrote, until it was time for a microwaved dinner. She wished that she could go to school every single day so she could have more homework.

Sometimes he barged into her room and said, "Stop it."

"What are you talking about?"

"You know what I'm talking about."

"No, I don't."

He pointed to the scribbled drafts on her desk. "You keep rewriting things over and over again. I've been watching you."

"You said you wanted a perfect report card."

He grabbed her wrists. "Get down on your knees."

*

Exhausted and relieved that the shadow had left her alone for a round of drinks with his buddies at Harriet's Bar down the highway, Olivia stood naked in the shower, begging the hot water to melt her body enough to disappear into the drain. When that failed, she put on her winter jacket and ran outside to the two-lane county highway in front of the house. Salt had been sprayed all over to give the ice some traction. She closed her eyes and walked straight ahead without paying attention to the sparse traffic. There she slipped on a patch of ice while trying to cross the highway. She didn't get up. She longed to feel the coarseness of salt burn up her face. She prayed that a truck would skid across her body, but when she heard two cars stopping and the voices approaching her, she screamed, "Leave me alone. Just let me die!"

This time she stayed longer at Treesburg. She didn't go back to school for three weeks.

Mitchell had volunteered to bring her homework every other day.

They sat together silently in front of the big window. Her crow was perched alone on its branch, its eyes zeroing onto her companion.

"I like crows," Mitchell finally said.

She looked up at her crow. "Yeah. Me too."

"They're supposed to be very smart. There's like thirty different kinds of 'em."

"Really? I didn't know that."

"Yeah."

A moment later she turned to him. "Do they talk about me at school?"

He nodded.

"Are you gay?"

"Why?"

"I don't like guys and I don't like girls, so what does that make me?"

"I don't know."

The following fall he transferred to a different school out of state.

*

When the shadow entered her, she willed herself to die each time. She returned to school feeling less of herself. Yes, she looked all there with her pretty clothes; Dad made a point of buying anything she wanted. Her antidepressants made her feel detached. She didn't feel the burnt pangs of blackness like before; they were merely frosted over with the icing of sweetness. Every day between classes she walked to her locker, swapped textbooks, and entered her next classroom early. She learned to smile coyly at everyone, but she never made conversation. The air of mystery—*why exactly did she want to die?*—added an aura to her beauty, and boys secretly ached for her even though they called her that "suicide chick." Teachers gave her a sympathetic look, yearning to say, *If there's anything I can do to help,* please *let me know.*

Classmates looked at her with a hidden fear. Even when teachers tried to encourage them to take turns in pairing up with her on in-class projects, they maintained a cool distance.

At home she made sure she was never alone with Dad. She refused to eat her meals with him anywhere. When she needed to be alone outside, she ventured to the dense woods behind their house. She took along her binoculars and sat still for long periods of birdwatching.

*

Olivia was surprised when Dad pressed the garage opener to reveal a used 1987 Honda Civic. The small car was white. Its rust spots had been sanded out and repainted. Its interior was red. Its hood had a big white bow.

"What?" She looked directly at him.

He nearly jolted from her glare. It had been a long time since she looked into his eyes. "Well, this is your graduation gift. You'll need to get around when you're in college, so ..." He jiggled the keys.

She stood staring at the car. "Why?"

"You deserve this. I mean, you got a full scholarship!"

"No," she whispered. "No."

"What?"

"I don't want it." She left for the house.

That night she did not sleep. She was afraid that he would open that door and demand that she show him some appreciation of all he'd done for her, the crap he had to take on her behalf, always telling everyone she was doing great—

But the door never opened.

In the last few weeks before she took the bus north to Minneapolis, she slept during the day when he was away at work. She packed her clothes, bird books, and binoculars carefully so she wouldn't need him to drive her to college. When it was time for him to drop her off at the bus stop, she made sure that her smaller backpack sat between them in the front seat.

When the car stopped, she immediately hauled out her big suitcase, swung her backpack onto her shoulder, and showed her ticket to the bus driver without saying good-bye to Dad. Once aboard, she chose a seat and closed her eyes for twenty minutes. She did not want to see Albert Lea again. She wasn't sure how, but she knew she was never coming back. The sight of endless farmlands greeted her eyes. She scanned the skies with her binoculars and noticed a murder of crows flying together as if they were following her. Had her crow told them about her?

*

Once settled at the University of Minnesota, she felt safe in the vast anonymity of a huge campus. She felt drawn to the ornithology classes where faculty and students, all of them bird lovers, gathered. She loved listening to them talk about the birds they'd sighted and researched.

No one looked at her lecherously. When she confessed her interest in crows, she felt welcomed into their midst. "Of course, crows are the best," one said. "What's your name again?" When she wasn't reading zoology textbooks, observing birds

in their cages and habitats, and writing term papers, she liked being alone on her bed in the dark. No music. Just silence. She left the window drapes open in case her crow wanted to look in on her. She allowed herself to wonder the questions she'd been afraid to ask out loud: what had made him feel so entitled to touch her like that? Even though she was quite model-beautiful, she nevertheless felt ugly; that she knew how to wield makeup didn't matter. Men noticed her, but she never returned their glances. She wasn't a lesbian, but the walls inside her were still on fire. A female gynecologist examined her and said that she could still have babies if she wanted them. "No thanks," she mumbled. She was forever pregnant with fear.

*

After Olivia earned her Ph.D. at the U of M, she found a teaching job in Duluth, a two hour-plus drive north of Minneapolis. She didn't like the city at first; it didn't have even a quarter of Minneapolis's population. Its steep streets were sometimes difficult to navigate; its winters were long and bitingly cold. But she loved the majestic view of Lake Superior from the big window of her apartment in Piedmont Heights. She never tired of looking at the lake, especially with her binoculars where she could pick out the types of gulls and birds sailing above the water.

She first noticed Scott, a marine biologist, at a faculty mixer hosted by the university. He wore a striped Oxford shirt that had seen better days and a pair of jeans that hinted at weeks of observations on Lake Superior where he drew water samples and captured fish for testing to ensure that the lake's pollution levels were still dropping. Although his dense beard hid his mouth, it was easy to tell whether he was smiling by the way his cheeks lifted. They didn't say much to each other at first, but the fact that he kept smiling encouraged her to ramble on. She surprised herself when she turned to Scott. "We should get together sometime." It was the most outrageous thing she'd ever said in her entire life.

"Sure."

They met again at a coffeehouse not far from the lake. After twenty minutes of idle chat, he said abruptly, "Can we, uh, go down to Canal Park?"

As the fog of dusk rolled around them on the shore, he seemed to come alive. He rhapsodized about the things he'd learned from the biology of water. Preferring to research, he hated having to teach four classes per semester. He wasn't a big fan of people. He said this was why he rarely dated. "I know it sounds kinda weird, but I'm, uh, an asexual. I like women, but I don't have any desire to, you know."

"'Asexual'? What's that exactly?"

The more he expounded on the subject of asexuality, the more she was surprised that such a community existed. Asexuals were rarely interested in sex; some of them preferred dates that ended in cuddling with clothes on. Was there indeed a label for her feelings?

"You okay?" he suddenly asked.

"I'm fine. It's just …"

He looked intently at her. "I don't talk about this, but I had things done to me when I was young. I'm on antidepressants, so I can't …" He gestured an index finger swinging upward.

She moved closer. "I think I understand."

That weekend he came over to her place for dinner. Even though her efficiency studio was tight with tall bookshelves crammed with textbooks and research studies, she'd never felt the need for more space. She liked its nest-like vibe, but when she allowed him inside, she felt suddenly embarrassed at how tiny it was.

"Hey," he said. "You okay?"

"Well, this isn't fancy."

"This is a lot nicer than mine. Seriously."

They sat at the small table and talked quietly. She'd made a vegetarian pasta casserole.

The meal done, he stood up and said, "Can we, uh, cuddle?"

She was surprised to see him wearing a red union suit underneath his clothes. It was a cold rainy night after all. She went into the bathroom and put on her flannel pajamas. Together in bed they inched together underneath the thick blankets. Once clasped around each other, though, they didn't let go. She was surprised not to feel an erection. She felt as if he was hanging onto her off the top of a storm-entrenched cliff. His deep breathing lulled her into sleep.

The morning after he said, "Last night was the best sleep of my life. Thank you."

They ate hot oatmeal and smiled awkwardly at each other in the gray light of dawn.

"You're really beautiful," he said. "You know that?"

She shook her head no. "People say that all the time, but I don't think—"

"Shh." He pushed his chair away from the table and opened his arms. "Come here." Afraid and yet not, she knelt before him and rested her head on his chest. She felt his hands stroke gently up and down her back. *Could a man be this kind and not demand her body?* She burst into sobs.

*

They bought a small house overlooking Lake Superior. They set up four birdhouses in their backyard, where a variety of birds converged especially in winter; they liked watching them from their kitchen window each morning. A small group of crows took to congregating on the thick telephone wires hanging near their garage. She waved at them every morning before she got into her car for work. It was not long before she could pick out some of their distinct personalities and named them Rascal, Carrie, Bicker, Nudge, and Nosy. Neighbors knew her as the Crow Lady.

In their home Scott set up two large aquariums in their living room. He said they were more relaxing than television. Some nights, when they were worn out from teaching, they cuddled underneath a heavy comforter and watched the fish shimmer brilliant flashes of color among the undulating plants. They fell easily into a deep sleep.

Even though they lived together, they never saw each other naked. Their house had two bathrooms so they showered separately. She couldn't remember being this happy or feeling so safe with another person.

*

Olivia, nearing forty, learned of Dad's death when his attorney left a voice mail at her work number. He had found her contact information online. A day later he called again, pleading her to return his call. Her father had left everything to her. The funeral would take place in five days. She knew the kind of lies people would likely spout in her father's name: loyal worker, devoted husband, proud father. Albert Lea seemed like a lifetime not hers; she had purged her hometown from her memory. Yet it had belonged to her. After his third voice mail asking her to please come down and figure out what to do with the house, she left a message on Scott's voice mail—"I need to disappear for a while but don't worry, okay?"—and drove the two hundred and fifty miles south into the evening. In the moonlight, her father's house's smallness looked strange and familiar. She'd kept the house keys; she wasn't sure if they still worked. Two clicks later, she was inside. She did not need a flashlight; her body had long memorized the layout inside. She had dreamed about this house too many times. The air felt different, almost heavy with dust, but she could still breathe. In the living room, she avoided the decrepit sofa and stood in front of where the TV used to stand. The statuette wasn't there.

She glanced elsewhere. It had been moved to the mantel above the fireplace. She carried it close to her bosom outside to her car. She arrived home four hours later and sat down in front of the kitchen window. In the early morning's light, she peered closely at Paul Bunyan's face. She was startled to find a hairline streak of white where the tear had dribbled. Had it been her imagination, or was it always there?

Scott, freshly dressed for the day, entered the kitchen. "Hey, Liv, you okay? Where were you?"

She set the statuette on the table and took a deep sigh. "I need to tell you something." In that first moment of release into the air, her faltering words about the shadow struck her how stories, when left untold, were indeed the most powerful of all. She looked at Paul Bunyan, and somewhere in its appearance was the promise of a story more outlandish than the last. This time, she decided, she would replace that empty promise with the rawness of her own story. No more celebrating the men who took whatever felt like theirs, no more excusing them who hid their sins long enough to score a loving tribute. No more silences. She knew exactly what she'd say in an email to the editor of *Albert Lea Tribune*: "For six years, my father Paul Albert Bishop (1957-2017) sexually molested me starting when I was 12 years old. I will not give him a tombstone. He doesn't deserve to rest next to my mother. Please don't ever honor his memory." She would ask her doctor if she could taper off her antidepressants.

When she was done telling, she looked up at Scott. Tears were trickling down his face. It was then they noticed a few crows clustered on the deck railing outside their window. She grabbed the statuette and a gas fireplace lighter from the counter next to the stove, and they walked outside to the firepit. The birds did not leave the railing; merely cocked their heads to watch.

She flicked the gas lighter a few times before its blue flame shot out. She aimed it at the statuette's base. Once the fire inched upward, she dropped it into the firepit. As the statuette turned charcoal-black in an acrid smoke, she began to feel light-headed when she watched each crow, one by one in turn, leap off the railing and take flight.

She laughed. "Yes!" She finally had wings.

David Patt
Covid Time

e may never know who was the first passenger to step off a plane at JFK or SEATAC bearing the innovative invader in her throat, an itchy throat that just had to cough a few times to spray a mist of replicating RNA onto innocent passersby who would in turn serve the virus on its journey to world domination via a simple algorithm of spit and exponential math. Anyway, it probably wasn't just one person, but a small but steady stream of arrivals from China or Italy. If that first infected person had not brought the novel coronavirus to the USA, it was only a matter of time before the second person, or the third, would have.

SARS-CoV-2 is a patient beast, not in a hurry to transmit it's offspring to the next human vector, but operating in in its own time, always ready to seize the moment when an unmasked cough introduces its invisible joyriders to a socially proximate inhaling human being. In fact, when the medical books are all researched and written, the one pervasive symptom of Covid-19 that may be omitted in the long list of syndromes is the remarkable ability of the virus to bend time.

On the macro level what we are talking about here is the blunt superpower to pretty much make the world stop. The natural world of course doesn't give a damn about the virus because the sun keeps rising, the grass grows when the rain falls, and the lioness carries on with her determined hunt for a fresh meal. But the human calendar, let's face it, has been thoroughly fucked. The school terms, conferences, concerts, sporting events, holidays that mark the rhythm of human culture—all erased or diminished to digital cartoons of themselves.

Work stopped. Weekends stopped. Knowing what day of the week it is became useless. Traffic as quiet at rush hour as it used to be only in the middle of the night. Night owls binged Netflix until drooping eyelids or sheer guilt made them press the pause button at 2:00 or 3:00 in the morning. Morning people still woke up early but what the hell, lay about with their phones reading the latest insights from The Atlantic and drinking coffee until Governor Cuomo came on the TV to tell us all how steep the mountain was and how soon we are all going to die.

Of course the bending of time, brought to the world's attention by the virus and its nemesis, the quarantine, was not actually a new set of circumstances, but a sudden cleansing of the doors of perception, allowing society *en masse* to perceive the unreliability and, to be perfectly honest, the ultimate unreality of time itself as a thing that is findable in any way other than as a conventional designation agreed upon by the world of humans, and then imposed upon ourselves as the responsibility to work from 9:00 to 5:00, gather with family at Christmas, and take a vacation in August.

Covid Time

Two thousand years ago the Buddhist philosopher Nagarjuna pointed out that there is no ultimately existent measurable unit of time. In conventional usage I can speak of past, present and future, and you know what I mean, but if we look beyond the words to determine if they refer to something that really exists we discover that such discreet temporal units are logically untenable. Experience tells us that present and future things must depend on past things. But how can something in the present have any relationship to the past unless it is in the past. To have any meaning, past and present must be different from each other, discreet temporal units. But in that case, how can a past thing have any relationship to a present thing? Past and present cannot have any connection with each other, and if they do, the past must be in the present and the present must be in the past. In our conventional language the *terms* past, present and future are completely dependent upon each other for their meaning. But if the temporal units they appear to refer to exist as real things in the world, they can never exist simultaneously, and therefore they cannot have any relationship, they cannot be dependent on each other. The conclusion is that we construct an orderly sense of time with the building blocks of conventional language, but under examination, it is a castle built on air—our conception of time, it's units and direction, are logically impossible.

Moving from the philosophical to the physical, it was early in the 20th Century that Albert Einstein and other physicists overturned the Newtonian conception of absolute time as an independent aspect of objective reality which progresses at a constant pace. Einstein's theory of relativity tells us that the clocks here on planet earth will tic toc and tell their story faster than the clocks of rocket-man hurtling through the cosmos, and the faster he flies the slower time passes on his rocket in relation to our earth-bound clocks. As rocket-man approaches the speed of light, the rate of time approaches zero. For massless particles like photons traveling at the speed of light, time has no effect. As the clock ticks here on earth, a photon leaving the sun will take 499 seconds or about eight minutes to reach our eyes. But if you could put a clock on the photon, it would show that it took no time at all to make the journey—it was instantaneous.

Time distorted and disorienting and unhinged from reliable regularity is not merely a side effect of the Covid pandemic; not so much a symptom of disease as an opportunity to glimpse the world as it really is. In the routine of the world before Covid the antibodies to this disorientation are ordinarily strong within us, in the form of habituation to the clock and calendar; moments of awakening to the relativity of time only appear in glimpses, momentary enlightenment experiences revealing how time is a socially constructed reality; that the predictability of routine events is an illusion, and that in the end, the only time that matters is the moment we are in right now (which, by the way, is already over).

Manila

In early March, when we all reluctantly began to grasp that a mindless microbe was going to bring global civilization to a halt, I was living with my partner in the Philippines, above her paint store on an impossibly gridlocked and noisy commercial boulevard. I was planning to return to the U.S. in April, but on the morning of March 17, I awoke to the news that as of midnight on Friday, March 20, Manila Airport would be closed to all international flights in and out of the country. I stared at the computer screen: if I was going to leave, it would have to be the next morning. Should I stay or should I go? Make a decision, right now. To leave so suddenly felt like I was deserting my adopted family. But if I didn't use this narrow window to depart, I might not get another chance. The virus was not yet rampant in Manila, but if I got sick, and the early projections made it seem more likely than not, did I want to be near hospitals in Boston, or take my chances in Manila? I had confidence in the training and professionalism of Filipino doctors and nurses. But the Philippines is a poor country, and there is no way that the resources could match what would be available if I ended up in critical care. Finally, decisively, I remembered that my travel medical insurance was going to expire in a month—I had to go. An hour after I woke up, I was packing. Twenty-four hours later I was on the way to the airport. The trip to the airport, which had taken two hours in gridlock hell six months earlier, took fifteen minutes. I was living in Covid time.

Boston

I was supposed to start work as an Enumerator for the U.S. Census in April, but Covid had other plans. The Census Bureau was reduced to a primitive website that informed its recruits that the constitutionally mandated counting of all the people in the country was suspended until further notice; please check back later for updates. As Robert Heinlein revealed to us in *Stranger in a Strange Land*, "Waiting is." I can't very well account for the next three months other than to say that I finally watched all five seasons of *The Wire*, and I learned more about epidemiology and immunology than I ever expected to care about.

Then in August the Census started. Having a work schedule felt comforting. I slipped into a rhythm of punctuated tedium, ringing bells and knocking on the doors of empty houses, one after another, when suddenly a door would open and there would stand an Ethiopian woman with four children playing in the background; after listening to the reasons the census is important to bring resources to our city, she would cheerfully recount the hard-to-spell names and birthdates and genders of all the members of her family.

After four months of isolating with my sister in her Boston apartment, communicating with friends only via phone and computer, stepping off the sidewalk into the street to give strangers a wide berth while on my daily walk, suddenly I was making direct human contact again, each day having friendly conversations with strangers. Though our faces were half-hidden behind masks, and always keeping what felt like a safe distance, for five- or ten-minutes people would sketch a quick portrait of the family life being lived behind their door. I found, in particular, that people living alone were happy to answer my questions and then linger, keep the conversation going, tell me something about the how the neighborhood had changed since they were a child, or that the house next door was empty because the couple decamped for Cape Cod to escape the pandemic, or that they had just retired after 30 years teaching Spanish in the public schools, with plans to return to Puerto Rico to spend the summer with her brother, who has health problems, but now it was too risky to travel.

The Covid wave had washed over the Northeast leaving refrigerated semi-trailers full of dead, but was now looking for fresh lungs in Florida and Texas and Arizona. In Boston the world was cautiously heading back to work, restaurants put seating out on the sidewalks, to cross major streets you had to actually wait for a green light because cars were back on the road. The daily rhythms of enumerating the census returned my mind and body to a sense of orderly time. Normal life, cautious, masked, safely distanced to be sure, seemed once again possible.

I was in a long, wide corridor in a new apartment building, designed like a massive hotel with studio apartments behind each door. As I slid a Notice of Visit under one door I saw down the hallway a woman who looked like a visiting nurse step out of an apartment where an elderly woman was holding the door open and saying goodbye.

"I'll see you in two days," the nurse said, "it's great to see you doing so well."

"Thank you for coming," the woman said. "It is always a pleasure to see you," and she closed the door.

I worked my way down the corridor and then looked down at my Census phone and saw that the next case was the apartment of the old lady. I knocked, and after a minute, from behind the door, "Who is there?"

"I am from the Census Bureau. Can you give me a few minutes so we can get you counted?"

"What do you want? Who are you?"

"From the United States government. We need to count everyone in the country. It will only take five minutes."

The door opened a bit and the woman stuck her head out. I stepped back to give us distance and held up the ID badge hanging around my neck. "I'm from the U.S. Census Bureau. In the Constitution it says that every ten years we have to count everyone in the country. The more people we count in Boston the more resources we get from Washington for medical care, senior care, hospitals and schools. Can I just ask you a few questions?" I said.

"My English is not so good," she replied with a shy smile. "Maybe I cannot do it."

"The questions are simple," I said, smiling behind my mask. "I think you can probably handle it."

"Just a moment. I will come back. Just wait," she said, and left me holding the door ajar. I thought she was going to get a mask, as many people did, but she returned in a brightly colored floral robe, slightly threadbare, which she held closed with her arm across her body. She was already fully dressed when she opened the door, but the robe was apparently required to be appropriately dressed for a conversation with a strange man at her door.

Her name was Elizabeth, and she was 82 years old. Her thick long hair was swept up in a loose bun held by a large inlaid clip at the back of her head. Her skin was smooth, and her thin lips curved in a kind of ironic smile which broadened when I asked her gender. "I am sorry, I have to ask," I said, "are you female?"

"Yes, of course. Do you want to see?" and she momentarily opened her robe, and we both started to laugh. She revealed nothing more than a thin old woman dressed in black slacks and a worn white blouse. But what I saw was a beautiful, slender seductress inviting her new paramour to glimpse the joys that lay ahead.

Her eyes twinkled at me and I felt like she was reading my mind, so I moved on, "Now just a few questions about ethnicity and we will be done."

"What is that? I do not know the meaning?"

"They want to know, do you consider yourself white, or black, or Asian. And then what is your background. What country do you come from?"

"Ah. I am Persian," she said with a pride and elegance that made me feel like she could have been the Shah's younger sister.

"Right," I replied, "I wasn't sure about your accent. My niece is married to an Iranian young man. Well, his parents are Iranian, he was raised in England and the US. How long have you been here in America?" We were finished with the census interview and now we were just talking.

"Would you like to come in?" she invited. "Perhaps I can give some water or some juice?"

It was a hot August day, I had been on my feet for hours, I was sweating, but I never said yes to such invitations. It was discouraged by our bosses, and after all, Covid made the rules now, this was an 82-year-old lady, and I was on the cusp of 70, neither one of us should be socializing with strangers. But Elizabeth had led me into Covid time, where the clock slowed down, and the present revealed itself as the only important moment.

"Well yes. I wouldn't mind a small glass of water if you have the time."

"Here we have some juice," she opened the refrigerator. "You would like some pomegranate juice? Or water?"

"Pomegranate juice sounds great," I answered, feeling that now I was surely entering the dream of a Persian princess.

She brought over a chair and we sat a safe distance apart. I realized that I had to remove my mask to drink the juice and asked if that was alright. A shadow of concern swept briefly across her face, but she nodded permission and I sipped the cool, tangy red nectar.

Elizabeth had sent her two children, a son and a daughter, to the U.S. to go to university. They both had moved into successful careers and in the early 1980's they had asked their mother to come join them. Her son, in fact, lived in the same building, a few floors above her apartment.

"You are more of a Bostonian than I am," I smiled. "I just moved here to live with my sister. I have one daughter working in England, and the other is in college. I just sold my house, so I am homeless right now."

"I have not seen my home in many many years," she responded. "Probably I will never see my beautiful country again. But I feel at home. I am here now. Where else should I be?"

I thought about the visiting nurse leaving the apartment a few minutes before. "And your health?" I asked. "Are you doing okay?"

"Ah," she sighed, "not so okay. Yes. No. I am good. But some chest. Some problems. Sometimes not too good. But I am happy. My son is upstairs. This is my life now. While I am here. This is our life now, isn't it?"

She looked me in the eyes, with her eyes twinkling, with her cascade of casually perfect hair, with her ageless skin, with her royal dignity. Time stood still. I wanted to stay. I wanted to listen to her exotic stories for a thousand and one nights. I wanted to invite her out to dinner at a fine restaurant with white tablecloths and well-dressed waiters. I wanted to make a new friend, to linger in the radiance of a Persian dream.

"Well I should go," I said. "Thank you so much for the delicious juice." I stood up and moved toward the door, I put my mask on. "I hope you stay healthy. Perhaps, someday in the future we will meet again."

"Yes," she smiled. "I would like that. Thank you for coming to my house. I am thankful for your visit. It was very nice."

I walked across the modern lobby and out into the bright sunshine of a summer afternoon. I looked at my census phone with its long list of non-responders and non-existent addresses. Three hundred and thirty million people to count, and I had taken too long, just counting one. But no one would ever know, because I had been counting in Covid time.

Mercury-Marvin Sunderland
Two Poems

Chapstick
chapstick
goes easy on those dry lips
heals a wound of cracked skin
which keeps getting ripped open

chapstick
is your daily reminder that you don't drink
    enough water
that you are constantly parched but forget you
    are dying of thirst

this medicine
is labeled with *tropical* flavor
which is vague as shit
but you put it on anyway
and notice how much
you want to eat it instead

even though your stomach is aching

these lips
will be licked dry
from anything meant to help heal
because you are just trying to get through your
    day
but your eating disorder makes you want to
    consume

i know
that
lots of people try to eat chapstick
and that doesn't inherently mean they have pica
but i do

and maybe
my addiction to eating things that aren't edible

isn't nearly as bad as it used to be
i know it might sound funny to you but

i remember those days
when i was addicted to eating plastic
because i knew it would kill me
and i wanted to die so badly

i remember constantly going through my day
while my head had the sensation of an inside-
    out plastic spoon
and oh, how i tried to laugh
at what i was using to kill me

i remember
difficult mornings
as i put on that chapstick
and faced yet another day
where i would eat my suicide

this evening
i put on chapstick
and drink from a plastic bottle of water

my hands
are not shaking

i line my lips and

i don't lick them this time.

Frozen Berries

frozen berries
take time to thaw but
it's morning and
you need to eat and

you don't care about that
brain freeze

frozen berries
taste like dessert
without that guilt but
you're too tired to
correct yourself on
feeling guilt for
what you eat

frozen berries
are a part of your breakfast this
morning and
not like how
not eating
was a part of your every lunch

frozen berries
taste sweet but
stain your fingers

your mom said
that eating disorders
make people lose their periods

you said
it was magazines

but really
you'd wanted to starve those fem curves out of
    your trans body but
it never worked

frozen berries
will bring a harsh memory
to your breakfast today.

Roger McKnight
Victoria

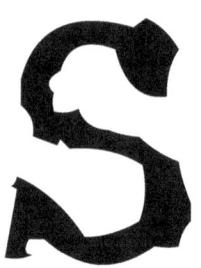ylvia Glasgow remarked, "Valencia isn't Ivy League, but better," then wondered if she meant it. As an alum, she loved her college, but a year on the road recruiting students for it tested her resolve. Today a delayed flight from Logan had prevented her reaching MSP early, so she was quickly pulling up facts about a Miss Larson, this morning's first interviewee, while giving her the standard introduction. "We're seeking serious students for a college with conscience."

Sylvia gathered her thoughts and studied the young woman, who had emerged from Starbuck's noontime throng and introduced herself as "Victoria—Tori, for short." She was thin-lipped and looked self-effacingly sly. Yes, that was Sylvia's first impression or, on second thought, maybe more like calm and self-contained. Like me, too, as an incoming freshman, way back when, she thought. I stayed quiet at Valencia in those days and let others label me as they wished.

"Sorry for the crowded setting," Sylvia continued after filing her reactions away and wishing desperately for the coffee she'd ordered. "My schedule's mad. Snowing in Boston. Snarled traffic in Minneapolis. But I so wanted to see you."

Tori nodded. "You just flew in?"

Sylvia said yes. "You? Any trouble getting here?"

"I drove. From home."

"Which is where? Let's see."

Sylvia searched her info for Tori's hometown, but she was left wondering where Minneapolis ended and St. Paul began. The Mississippi wound in and out between the communities and local maps seemed created to obscure the city limits.

"It's the burbs," Tori replied, as if reading Sylvia's mind and trying to simplify the answer.

"Yes," Sylvia agreed. "You're from Golden Valley."

"No, Apple Valley."

"Right. To the southwest."

Tori's slight smile failed to show whether Sylvia was right or wrong. "Close enough," she said, which Sylvia took to mean 'no matter.'

"And you're at Central High?" Sylvia asked. "Don't get many apps from there."

"No secret why not," Tori explained. "Inner city hood, rubbing elbows with Latinos. Blacks. Boat people. I had a boyfriend, one of *them*. My folks said no."

"No to what? Him or Central?"

Tori nodded without saying which, so Sylvia assumed she meant both. At last a barista appeared and put down a cappuccino for Sylvia, who nodded to Tori. "Your turn. My treat," Sylvia said, relieved to skip the intricacies of Metro geography.

"Light brew, tall," Tori ordered while looking steadily at Sylvia. "My dad's company, Villospor, is close. I used that to argue for Central, going to classes near his job."

"So your father's employed at Villospor?"

"Kinda owns it."

While Tori added cream to her light brew, Sylvia talked community service. "Valencia's moving from theory to awareness to engagement, all for the common good." She stirred her cappuccino, then chose a napkin and delicately wiped a smudge from her cup, which she saw Tori observing with a slight twist of her mouth but a neutral expression.

"Sorry," Sylvia said. "My germ phobia."

"Lots have 'em, I'm immune," Tori replied. She described her volunteer job at the Humane Society, where weird microbes flourished. Caring for abandoned or feral cats was her task. "I found four scrawny kittens dumped under some football bleachers. Lots of fleas and claws. They scratched me. See?"

"Heavens," Sylvia exclaimed. She applauded Tori for the rescue but was taken aback by the length of the bandage covering her arm.

Tori lifted the gauze, so some still-moist blood ended up on her hand. "Dear creatures," she said while wiping off the stain. "What you see in their eyes is what they have in their hearts. Sorry that sounds so dramatic, heard it in a movie the other day."

Sylvia jotted notes while glancing at the girl's injured arm and rechecking her high school transcript. Encouraging her to talk on, Sylvia said "yes, yes," and wondered what to expect next.

"My ex is a like a kitten. He woulda been in college now."

"He was your boyfriend?"

"Name's Pancho. Long gone."

Sylvia wondered about 'gone' but avoided prying. "You've got good grades," she observed. "Any exciting classes?"

"Spanish. Our teacher's TexMex. Señor Gonzalez. Gonzo. Speech is great, too. Learning to get ideas across."

"Fantastic. Valencia's new curriculum emphasizes communicating across boundaries. Demographics are shifting," Sylvia explained. She resisted delving into the anomaly of Valencia reaching out to the poor while recruiting the rich.

"I took a mini-course on digital literacy and fake news," Tori replied, as she nodded okay to a refill from the barista, who spilled a tiny portion. Tori swiped at the excess and licked it from her finger with a flourish. Sylvia wondered if the gesture showed the young woman's ease in her presence or boredom with her questions.

"Sorry, me and my boyfriend had that habit," Tori explained. "Licking."

"At Valencia we're taking theory and practice to the community," Sylvia continued while filing away the girl's words. "Explaining complex ideas in everyday language."

"Speaking well's a must," Tori agreed.

"We're located back East. Lotsa nor'easters. Some want palm trees."

"Cool and breezy here, too."

"Other schools on your agenda?"

"Hanford. In San Fran. Went there with my dad. He bought a cottage at Nob Hill. Least 'cottage' is what he calls it. We stayed there, Thanksgiving and Christmas."

"Yes, great campus," Sylvia responded enthusiastically.

"Cal State's better."

"Two very different places."

"My ex, he was going to go there."

"Cal State?"

Victoria nodded yes.

Sylvia considered their differing sentiments about the California universities and wondered again about Tori's boyfriend being gone. She guessed at a disagreement between daughter and father. Did Tori prefer state universities because of her boyfriend or their counter-culture reputation?

"Dad says Nob Hill to impress people," Tori continued. "The cottage is on a hill, all right, but no nob. He makes tons buying warehouses and storing stuff for companies. Dreams of buying his way into uppity places."

"Valencia features study abroad. Interested?" Sylvia asked, seizing her chance to move on.

"My family was in Biarritz. And a month in Tahiti. Mom even went along. French is lovely."

"I spent a year in Grenoble, as an exchange student," Sylvia said, happy to pick up the ball. "The Alps and trips to Paris. Changed my life. My French prof always said the French are the most intelligent people on our planet."

"I liked their language better than the guys who spoke it. Way too grabby."

Sylvia said, "Yes, gladly," when the barista offered her yet another refill. The coffee simmered as she jotted *not your usual scholar* in her notes and wondered where they were heading. Sylvia's eager attempts at promoting the great wide world plus the chance to study at a prestigious school had given Tori no impetus to explain her goals. Maybe, Sylvia pondered, she's already been there, done that. At eighteen? And what would I know about such privilege? Me, an ex-scholarship girl Valencia's sending out to hustle in big bucks, hopefully with brains to match?

"Let's be frank," Sylvia decided to say. "Generations of bookers have kept Valencia steeped in tradition. We're searching." Whoa, wrong word, she caught herself thinking. "Actively seeking."

"I know, something new," Tori interrupted. "I'm an intuitive learner." She paused as though intuitive learner was something she'd said before, or heard somebody else say, without ever finding a concrete theme to match it with. "Like your college, I'm looking for an answer." Tori waved her half-empty cup back and forth as if to put her wording in perspective. Nothing spilled.

Unable to locate any nugget in Tori's words that Valencia's tuition-driven staff would find promising, Sylvia blurted out, much like a schoolgirl, "Study habits? Any nook or cranny, where you go to get schoolwork done? Vent, in silence? To cool it?"

A bemused smile flitted across Tori's face. Probably at my word choice, Sylvia thought. *Chill* is what youngsters say nowadays, she remembered. Tori's reaction made Sylvia think of her husband Michael's patient reaction when fielding their children's innocent questions at home.

"Not really. Like the testers say, I'm a creative learner," Tori answered.

Intuitive learners don't look for places to study, Sylvia realized, because they never study, at least not systematically like the goal-oriented brains Valencia's reputation rests on.

"Creative, meaning what?" she asked Tori, determined to carry on.

"I hear the questions and put my label on them after they're all in."

"So you wait for people to present their ideas and then decide if there *is* a question?"

"Kinda," Tori agreed. She ran a finger around the rim of her coffee-stained saucer and licked it once more. "Or if the question's worthy of attention."

"So if there is a serious question, you decide to start studying?"

"That's when I decide to look for better answers."

What was left of Sylvia's cappuccino cooled, so she sipped at it distractedly while Tori watched the noon-hour crowd filtering off to their workplaces. In her notes, Sylvia wrote *well-placed family, has traveled,* but she was only scribbling. Mostly she wondered why Tori reminded her of herself at that age, despite the obvious gap in their families' wealth. Maybe Tori's way of smiling from a distance at the busy downtowners was an expression of sympathy, as if she imagined the office workers scurrying back to a demanding boss, not unlike her own father. Sylvia remembered herself as a booker, though not the kind who buried herself in the stacks at Valencia's hallowed library. She did her lessons in cozy cafés and studied passersby, in Tori's style, she guessed.

"Sorry, not your usual interview, I know," Tori said in a soft tone, half question and half apology, which interrupted Sylvia's wandering thoughts.

Interviewer and interviewee scrutinized each other, gradually rendering transparent the hazy filter separating them. Sylvia asked in confidence, "Central High. Why?"

"I told you. Pancho."

"And his real name? C'mon."

Being detected for concealing her boyfriend's name caused Tori to quiver, slightly. Sylvia felt equally uncertain for having asked about it. Calling out an applicant for a white lie isn't a sin, she reflected, but not part of my job either. Nevertheless, Mr. Larson's social climbing, measured against his daughter's caring kitten rescue, suggested some discord in their family, however trivial it might seem. Sylvia guessed the relationship was based on strong love between father and daughter, which nurtured Tori in the frequent absence of her mother, whose maladies Tori had alluded to in her application essay.

Sylvia guessed Mr. Larson's strength of will showed up in Tori after she started school, but in ways the father least expected. Tori had written of taking change from her little brother's piggy bank as a ten-year-old and treating her friends to candy and pop because the poor kids got no allowance. Yes, even in suburbs the permanent underclass and unregistered immigrants were present and eked out their living as maids and day laborers, Sylvia knew. In high school Tori joined diversity groups, as her essay proudly detailed. If those extra-curriculars took the father by surprise, he could tolerate them as a youthful whim. Sylvia imagined the falling-out over Tori's social preferences reaching a head when she brought Pancho home to meet her parents.

"His real name's Chino," Tori admitted. "His family's from Guatemala. They've lived here since he was a baby. He taught me Spanish."

Images flitted through Sylvia's mind of Tori and Chino dallying at school in Spanish. Such scenes may have troubled her father. That vision gave Sylvia pause as well, but not because she judged Tori for it.

Before Sylvia could carry the thought further, the baristas began clearing tables. She and Tori were the only customers left. "My next applicants are in Park Center, wherever that is," she announced.

"We were doing okay, me and my dad," Tori continued, seeming not to hear Sylvia's words. "He wasn't happy about Pancho, but I handled it. Least till Dad voted for Trumpkopf. Now he's in Washington kicking Latinos out in the street."

Sylvia hesitated. She wondered whether to break her Admissions Office rules and discuss politics or say 'Sorry' and move on to other interviews with her trusty GPS.

"You're looking for Oro Park plus Oro Center. That's Park Center for short. North from here," Tori explained, again appearing to read her interviewer's thoughts.

"So why call your boyfriend Pancho?" Sylvia asked.

"We met in Phy Ed tennis. He was so good, always hit the sweet spot," Tori replied, unable to hide a blush. "The teacher said some Latino named Pancho was this all-star, so Chino became Pancho."

"They didn't get along, he and your father?"

"Yes, no, nothing like that. Pancho's polite to his elders," Tori said intently. "Dad's a push-over, long as you toe his line. He looks the other way hiring at Villospor. The feds are always checking on him. There were considerations."

"Meaning?" Sylvia wondered.

"Meaning don't tread on Dad's space. He takes it personal."

A guy with Nob Hill in his dreams found it unbearable, Sylvia guessed, having the government interfere with his business or a Latino call the shots with his daughter. Mr. Larson could live with Pancho's family in the workplace, but nowhere else. That issue weighed on Tori's mind, but the more she discussed her seemingly vague college plans the better Sylvia understood Tori was bending their conversation in a direction more pressing than her father's ideas about social standing.

"Dad didn't worry about Pancho," Tori continued. "Only the gangs. Knifings, drugs. Mexicans were meaner than Central Americans. He thought they'd go after Pancho."

"So what did he propose?"

"I said I could date who I wanted. Not under my roof, he said. Mom was already holed up in her sick-room, and Dad wasn't about to lose me, too. That's when the travel bug hit. For him, the lifelong workaholic, seeing the world was a dream, like another Nob Hill, as long as he could keep me close. France and Tahiti were cakewalks. We went to other places you wouldn't believe. Kangaroo Island, Kamchatka, Kiev. He took my brother shooting polar bears in Spitsbergen so I'd tag along. You think Boston's rugged, try Goodyearbyen. Or Nuuk."

Tori's voice rose, so she stopped in a hrmpph. "All this to make me forget a boy, which I wasn't about to do?"

Sylvia wondered the same, only the other way around. She recalled her own departure for France a decade-and-half earlier. Fearing her year abroad would cause Michael, then her college sweetheart, to forget her, she cried for days before parting. That memory gave her a twinge of conscience. Unlike Tori, she never encountered any grabby French guys, but fell for Youssef, from Bahrain, who said he was a political refugee in France. They met at a foreign-student reception in Grenoble and made love in student digs, Alpine resorts, and leafy parks by gurgling streams. While Michael waited at home, Sylvia freed herself from what Youssef called middle-class convention. In the long run, it was Sylvia who almost forgot Michael. Indeed, she would have done so, she was certain, if Youssef hadn't left his studies and returned to Bahrain, under the threat of prison at home. She and Michael got married after graduating from Valencia.

"So what do you want from Valencia?" Sylvia asked. Normally she used an interview's final minutes to discuss what the college and prospective student could give each other, but Tori remained so vague Sylvia narrowed the topic.

"Getting things right," Tori responded. "I picked Valencia when I read about your school's financial problems. Dad gave in to me. I said I'd never forgive him unless."

"And so, you reconciled?"

"You have no clue," Tori continued. "Pancho took a year off after Central, so Dad took him on at Villospor. Stock boy, to see what he's made of. That's when Pancho applied to Cal State. He knew what he wanted."

Sylvia peered out across the empty café. The quiet liberated her from worries of flight delays and scheduling. About Guatemala she knew only this and that. She once attended a lecture on Mayan weaving and dyeing. Otherwise she remembered disturbing reports of brutal attacks on Indian villages. Sylvia wondered if Pancho's relatives were among the casualties. Or were they the poor boys drafted into the Guatemalan police and taught to murder?

"But Pancho never made it to California?" Sylvia guessed.

"This country's hell, like Guatemala used to be. Latinos cower waiting for ICE to knock at the door and jerk them away."

"Trump says Latinos are 'bad hombres'," Sylvia replied and realized she had nearly crossed over into partisan politics.

"Pancho's little brother went around crying out 'Trump es malo. Why does he want to take my parents away?' His folks had to stop him from saying that at school, where you never know who's listening."

Noting Tori's switch to the past tense, Sylvia patched together a sequence: First Pancho applied to college in California and later on Tori began

looking, too. That's when talk started about building a wall on the border and word spread. If ICE pounds at your door, don't open it. If ICE appears without a warrant, don't answer them. If ICE asks your name, don't give it.

"Even my dad's aghast at the madness," Tori continued. "Pancho's folks went for their annual immigration review, but ICE put them in detention. Pancho had to sit down with his uncle and figure how to manage the household while his mom and dad were being held. He got a second job to keep up payments on their mortgage, and an aunt agreed to care for his little brother and sister.

"The authorities claimed the family had Indian blood. They're from a town called Verapaz. They're descended from German immigrants, and Pancho's got blue eyes. But even if they were Indians, why build a wall to exclude the continent's original inhabitants?"

Sylvia felt uncomfortable fielding questions containing their own answer. So she found herself searching for a sensible response and worrying again about her next interviews.

"There's yet more?" she asked, perfectly aware her own question answered itself.

"They deported them, all three," Tori replied, her emotions showing clearly for the first time. "Him and his parents. Gone. Pancho skyped me last night from Verapaz, he said the hardest part was how they took his parents 'away from their heart, their little children. It was the worst pain. Like they were dead.'"

Sylvia thought about Youssef. Immigration authorities in France had treated him fairly, but common Frenchmen often looked askance at him. When Youssef returned to Bahrain, Sylvia said she'd go with him and naively imagined herself aiding his cause, which in truth she never understood.

"Your dad? What does he say?" Sylvia asked, fishing to plug the temporary lull between her and Tori.

"He did research that said getting rid of immigrants would set the U. S. economy back 15%. That tipped the scales for him. One hope was having Pancho brought back on a foreign student visa, but Cal State hadn't even read his application yet. Plus, Immigration insists he's an *indio*, and they won't allow him back as a foreign student because he's not a foreigner. Next'll be his brother and sister. Born here."

"So what's the question you've sorted out?" Sylvia asked. "Cal State, Hanford?" she asked cautiously.

"No way, it's Valencia or Verapaz," Tori said with a determined shake of her head.

Her composure made it unclear if she had arrived at Starbuck's determined to present that very ultimatum or if she'd just invented it, on the spot.

"Me below the border? Dad'd never dream of it," Tori went on. "But if Pancho can't come back here, I'll go there, hell or …"

Tori paused. "I'm begging you."

"To step in where others failed? Who am I?" Sylvia protested.

"Remember, a college with conscience?"

Sylvia thought how that phrase had drifted toward cliché even at Valencia as the drive for money took precedence at the college, and here was a co-ed with cash. If Tori chose Valencia, was it possible, getting the college to approach Immigration for Pancho? And if they'd do it for him, then others, too? Maybe, she allowed. A warehouse man's money spoke as loud as anybody else's, but how would the college use it? Actions spoke louder than words.

The two women looked each other in the eye. Sylvia wondered how things would have gone if she'd been as determined as Tori and followed Youssef back to Bahrain. Or did Youssef cunningly plan their relationship to end exactly when he was to leave France?

"Using me till the time was right?" she asked, only to realize she was talking aloud to herself. Anyway, she thought, life has turned out good, for me.

"C'mon, time to go," Tori said impatiently. "How'll you make Park Center alone? GPS?"

"You have a better answer?" Sylvia replied.

"I'll drive. I made you late to start with."

"My rental car."

"Follow me in it."

"The answer to my prayers," Sylvia said. Getting to Park Center on time made catching her flight home a cinch; Michael fared better with the kids any time she was on her way.

Sylvia paid the cashier. Approaching the car, she said, "Sorry, but I need to find my own way."

Tori halted. "They didn't name me Victoria for nothing," she said in determination.

"You have an interesting application," Sylvia explained guardedly. "Don't know what more I can say."

"I won't be stopped."

Sylvia held her car door open, one foot in the driver's side and the other planted outside it. When Tori stubbornly leaned against the front bumper, Sylvia sighed and got out. Thus deadlocked with the younger woman as the bleak winter sun gradually began sinking, Sylvia compared the two of them, privileged in different ways yet equally involved in others' woes. Slowly she let her guard down and smiled, first in dismay at the world, then sympathetically toward Tori, who returned the gesture.

They shared those smiles, until Sylvia checked the time again. "Okay," she said. "Let's give it a try. Talk to your dad. I'll do my best back East. No promises. We're not Ivy League, you know."

"No, but maybe better," Tori answered.

Sylvia got in the car, zapped her window down, and shook hands with Tori out through it. Driving off in a rush, she neglected the GPS. Soon she even lost track of which city she was in, Minneapolis or St. Paul, or where this Park Center could possibly be, but no matter, she consoled herself, as she oftentimes had done at confusing sites, every road eventually comes out some place good, for somebody. Continuing on with common sense to guide her, she wondered if good was always the same as right. She'd find out soon enough.

Imani Skipwith

The Palm of Death's Hand

er teeth grinding against each other, she moved slowly toward the window. The cigarette she held down burned her thigh in an attempt to delay her steps. Her brain said continue, but it also said stop. Confusion tugged at her hair and Death stood in front of her, holding her free hand, pulling her along. She stopped in front of her mirror and smiled crookedly. Her once delicate face was now cut up, and bruises kissed it forcefully. The bags clung to her eyes in fear of falling into themselves, her lips plumper than usual from eating at them every night. Her eyes burned with tears and the need to sleep washed over her. She didn't want to stop, though. She only stared into herself until the reflection wavered and rippled away—until there was nothing. She bit at her lip until the metallic taste of blood seeped into her mouth like water from a spring. She frantically tried to scribble the thought from her mind. In response, her purple legs fought to get ahead of each other, dragging her behind as they bickered about who'd get her to the window first. Her throat burned, and her vocal cords had been blown out. She tried to call for help, but there was no candle left to lighten up the dark abyss.

The Life in her body shrugged its shoulders and decided to take the elevator down to her feet, only stopping once to take in what they once called home. The heart was swelling, the lungs had shriveled, and the liver had flooded long ago but no one bothered to call a plumber. Why fix something that would continuously break itself over and over again. So, Life paid its lease to Death and abandoned her. Death grinned, infatuated, and wrapped his arms tightly around her waist. She desperately tried to push Death away, screaming at Life, offering to fix her vessel to become the proper home. Life only shook its head sadly and continued on its way as Death tangoed with her cries for help, fear, and desperation. He gingerly touched her face, and she flinched at the sandpaper feel, still begging. But Death is hard of hearing. He spun her around and dipped her from the ledge of the window. She became a waterfall, for her tears flooded the ground below. Death's breath was hot against her neck as he planted small kisses on her collarbones, shattering them with each peck.

She writhed in agony and poured her sorrows into the river below the small apartment window. The wind tugged violently at her hair and the lightning above kissed her forehead. The window shook at the sound of the thunder and descended. She shut her eyes, prepared to forever dance in the darkness or face whatever deity she may encounter. Suddenly, the wind stopped, and she felt herself drop onto something uncomfortable. There she was, sitting in one of her horribly cushioned chairs, staring Death in the eyes. He licked his lips and crouched in front of her.

"Are you afraid?"

"No," the girl lied, crushing her teeth together with squinted eyes.

Her bitten and broken nails dug into the chair as much as they could. Death cocked his head back, allowing his laughter to bounce off the walls and dance in the corners.

"Why do you lie, girl? I know just as well as you do how fearful you are. Were you not just begging Life to come back just a few minutes ago?"

She hesitated, feeling his eyes cut their way into her soul. He patiently waited for her response, joyfully watching her fumble with decisions and judgement. Silenced washed over the two. She nodded her head.

More laughter from Death. He lit a cigarette and plopped down on the hard chair in front of her, taking a long drag. He leaned forward with an amused smirk upon his face and kissed her cracked and scarred lips, filling her airways and lungs with clouds of endless smoke. Her lips started to grow cold and he placed the cigarette between them with a look of satisfaction in his eyes.

"Fausta. How come you're such an unlucky girl?"

Fausta laughed for the first time in a while and inhaled the nicotine, smiling up at the ceiling. "That's a question I could never find the answer to."

Death looked at her, perplexed. "Is that so, or are you just refusing to acknowledge the answer?"

She froze and looked down at her toes, pressing the cigarette lightly against the ashtray in front of her. Fausta shook her head and sat back further in the chair.

"I know you know the answer. You've always refused to accept it."

Fausta looked up at Death, irritation painted across her face. She barely flinched as she put the cigarette out on her forearm and stood closer to him until she could feel his breath against her eyebrows.

"How do you know that? Why're you even here?"

"You'll have to see me eventually. Life already abandoned you. Why not me?" Death chuckled and wrapped his arm around her shoulders, guiding her to the dimly lit windowsill. The moon glowed red and what once was a river of her tears, was now an alleyway; the only light came from an old street light that flickered every two minutes. She sighed, pressing her forehead against the window. "The world is so full of disappointment, Fausta. Filled to the brim with it. You of all people should know that. You should *also* know that it most definitely does not get better. In fact, you're

more vulnerable now that Life left you. Depression's got you wrapped around his little finger and Anxiety's jittery ass is right behind him. They've had their eyes on you since birth. Do you really think they'd let you go that easily? You can try as hard as you want to push them away, but they will never fully go away, sweetheart. How about this offer? Just let me help you. I'll give you exactly what you want. You'll never suffer again; I promise you that."

Death's hand searched for hers. Chills surged through her body. Her breath fogged the glass in front of her. She looked up at Death, helplessness written in her eyes, tears brimming, and she sighed.

"I don't need your help. I can do it on my own. This isn't for you or even about you. This is for my peace of mind. I wake up and I realize every single time that I'm not worth anything in life. I'm dishonoring everyone who had so many high expectations of me. All those canvases that just sat unfinished in that studio kept mocking me, all those unwritten songs and terrible music. All of it reminding me that there's no original talent in my bones. I'm just a child playing around with Dollar Store watercolors and fingerpaint. There is no way I could put on a completely successful art show. There is no way I can carry out a successful concert. No. Way. This is *my* escape."

"But Fausta, *I'm Death*. You carry this out and you'll see me, regardless. Whether you want it to be about me or not, it's still going to end up being all about me. Not to be a narcissist, but once it's about me, it's *all* about *me*."

"Is that so?" Fausta's eyes hardened, and her soul turned to stone.

She lit another cigarette and proceeded to fill the entirety of her body with sickness, all the while glaring at the tall being in front of her. Getting up from her spot on the windowsill, she blew the fear that she'd breathed in from the cigarette smoke out into his face and anger circulated through her heart. Cigarette between her lips, she walked back to the mirror and plastered that same signature, crooked smile onto her face. Something was different this time, though. There was something more sinister behind it. It looked more helpless than before; more broken.

Death just sat and stared at the damaged soul in front of him, pleading for help that he only knew one way to provide. To his surprise, Fausta started to pound her fist into the mirror, smashing it continuously. Then she flung it onto the floor. Blowing out a puff of smoke, she sped to the bathroom, snatched open the cabinet door, reached inside and threw her prescriptions and medication across the room.

Fausta opened the pill bottles, pouring them out one by one while Death stood at the doorway, amused. Blood dripped on the floor, washing the pills on the ground. Taking a towel and wiping her hands, she pushed past Death and made her way towards the studio. Her musical instruments were neatly placed in cases and on racks on one side of the room. On the other side, canvases and large platforms of wood lay strewn about or sat on easels. One by one, she took out guitars, ukuleles and keyboards and threw them about. Angrily, she smashed easels through canvases, tearing the frames and skin. Once she was done, and the room looked as if a tornado and earthquake had happened simultaneously, she stood and examined the room, her breath heavy. Almost triumphantly, she looked over her shoulder at Death, a smug grin crossing her lips.

"There's nothing left of me in this house. I should've left a long time ago. Get out."

Death blinked and walked in front of her. He leaned down to peer into her, that same smug grin creeping onto his face. "I'm sorry, what did you say?"

"I said get out!" The smoke that she'd been inhaling seeped from her pores, anger stinging her eyes.

Death's lips formed into a grim, thin line. "Ah, I see. I guess I'll take my leave but are you sure you don't want to reconsider? Depression will come for you again, and this time he won't be so lenient."

"Tell him to do his worst."

D.E. Green
Four Poems

At the Shakespeare Conference
Death stalks this place. It's in the
panel on indigenous Shakespeare—
Dream translated into Mohawk and
Bottom into a moose—into dying—
languages—the scholar mourns
fewer than ten speakers left—*I
know when one is dead and when one
lives*—overwhelmed by loss— the
cross-dressing woman whose
father survived the Holocaust—lost
to her— the memory of the play—
about Sholem Asch and *his* play—
and myriad shadows—some my
own—dead—like Yiddish. *Yet who
would have thought the old man to have
had so much blood in him.* Languages

dying— and people—friends—
dying. Pretending—just dabbing my
eyes—the watery eyes we old folks
get.

Rooming—three decades—
with a friend—dead— a year
ago—his absence— present.
He's *dead as earth*. The
famous maze of L.A.'s
Bonaventure—the tower
wells—scholars milling
around Registration a floor
below—standing at a loss in
the lobby.
 Scholars beset by loss—
obliviousness—loneliness— how
did I miss it?

Fading rose blooms—*his eyes were
green as leeks*— arranged for
wedding— or for wake—the
petals' edges— brown—
dropping—now— again. Gone—
the baby's breath—its resilience.
Gone—the green ferns that set us
off—the hardy carnations—vital
as our middle age.

Everything—I hear, see—
speaks—languages of the
dead. Death has its own
tongue. Death— opulent
labyrinth— we cannot
escape. Over there—
Ariadne— her sister
Phaedra— hunched
together— but still—the
lively eyes. Theseus
hobbles— to his
Hippolyta—silent
now—no public tongue—
just quill and ink— hatched
parchment. Books occupy
less space— *nor I nor any
man that but man is*— the
publishers are dying— *with
nothing shall be pleased till he be
eased with being nothing.*

Death. Deaths. The dead—
pervasive—my own gray head—
gray hair—no hair— the mirror by
the elevators. (Death's other face is
mine.) The young—painfully
vibrant— *all the world's a stage*—I
strutted once—now theirs. Arc of
tragedy—our parts slighter—fewer
words— sporadic scenes—acts
end— with—or without—my
lines— (*I cannot remember my lines*)—
whether—or not—my character—
is ready. Perhaps—*look there*— my

grandfather again— we speak—in
Yiddish. Perhaps—my
grandmother— *look there*—lights—
Sabbath candles—with
grandmothers— before her—
whose names— I do not know.
Perhaps—I speak—Shakespeare in
Mohawk—*the rest is silence*—
tongue—lines of Ashbery—who
loved— Shakespeare—who loved.

Perhaps—*look there*—fragile bodies—
tender language.

Sestina: Song for the Apocalypse

We've reached the end. No
one is coming to save us. It's
far too late for that. The earth
will warm. The seas will flood
the cities and lap at our eyes.

We cannot turn away, shield our eyes,
pretend that this is not the promised end
or image of that horror, Noah's flood for
real this time. No savior will arrive to
succor us, to warm our hearts, quell our
fears. Later

we'll realize we knew it all. Later our lids
will flutter, our eyes roll back. We'll
know what warm means. We'll know
that Now is ending. We will rush
senselessly about to save
this or that knick-knack from the flooding

waters. And the past, the past will flood in, will
well up in us too late to do us any good. A
memory, comforting, save for the pain, for salt-
tears that inundate our eyes.
It is—face it squarely now—the end.
And it is, as scientists prognosticated, very warm.

You too are warm, alive,
facing the rising flood.
Cool to the end. Stalwart, steadfast,
like your late father, but with the fierce, keen eyes
of a mother, willing a remedy to save

a dying daughter, to sooth and save an infant
son, breath failing, skin barely warm. Even you
will then turn away, your eyes welling up, the
tear-flood spilling over: Our lament so late, so
near our end.

The very end—save for a belated sigh, a
last warm mist, a dew that floods our
vacant eyes.

A Palpable Hit

Nicked it—the deer in early
autumn darkness on a long
drive home. Damage minor:
Dented hood. Fear sprayed
along the driver's side of the
white Focus.

Your relief at my safety trumped
the deer's fate— I'm no longer
second fiddle to squirrels and
red-throated blackbirds that
swoop at the car between late-
summer cornfields.

That deer—the white rump in
the light moving too slowly
even as I brake, veer toward
the ditch. The deer dies or I
do. Kill or be killed.

It hits me: This world we
live—and die—in. I see it
now: the fact of nature,
our nature, visible—a
Confederate monument

in a town square, Mount
Rushmore on sacred
ground. It's always been
this way—sudden death
looming on a highway in
unaccustomed autumn
dark, so near home and
you.

Once More into the Breach

The gun must have gone off
without my even knowing
because you look wounded.

I always forget that there is no peace
treaty, just a demilitarized zone that
sometimes seems

like a quiet garden and sometimes like
the trenches of a Great War
battlefield—inescapable, hopeless.

What was it I said or didn't say? Was I
not listening closely enough to words
that mattered vitally

to you? Did I take them as incidental?
As casual? Did I forget that my voice
registers always, even now, as *father*?

Did I forget that is a name to conjure
with, a voice that speaks obliteration as
often as love, or even as it speaks

or means to speak love? Now I see it in
your face. Too late. I hear my words
again as I hear the words of my own

father, who loved me and failed to
love me in the ways I needed—
never enough and much too much.

Justin Watkins
Fish Moon

t the start of a quarantine they took each night the old aluminum canoe down to the abandoned quarry pond near their home. The pond was small with high banks such that most winds did not touch its surface. It ran deep with cold groundwater and in the spring rainbow trout rose steadily for the hours leading up to sunset: cruising and rising, snipping at bugs that were also rising. The man was always in the stern at the paddle and the boy in the bow, working a fiberglass fly rod. It was a spot-and-shoot approach: watch for a rise, lay the soft hackle just past the riseform and strip it slowly through. The eats were sudden and sometimes violent; some of the bigger trout would break the tippet on the hookset. If the light were just right, they could see the green backs of the trout at the water surface, marauding and hunting according to their own primordial codes and understandings. In this way it was hunters hunting hunters. As it's been and as it should be, the man would say.

On April seventh the water was at glass calm and the only sounds were careful movements echoed by the aluminum and the passing of the fly line in the air. The boy did not require prompts; he waited and watched and moved as needed. He had handed a number of trout back to the man, who killed each one by striking it with the pommel of his knife. There was blood on hands and on fly boxes and beer cans and it mixed with the water that dripped from the paddle blade down into the canoe. The blood came from the water and now it mixed with it at the man's feet and later the blood would become the man and the boy.

The sun moved below the treeline to the west and the moon was coming into view. They watched a rise and tracked the trout's movement as its dorsal fin cut through the water leaving slashes and swirls. The boy put one false cast to the side and then laid the soft hackle out to intersect the fish's path. The soft hackle they had made the night before and it was only colored thread and a grouse feather palomared around the hook shank. It lighted on the water and the boy had just started a slow stripping retrieve when the trout ate the fly. It jumped twice and they watched it flash in the clear water, side to side resisting the tension that drew it to the canoe. As the fish was landed the moon rose entire and the man and the boy both stopped what they were doing. It was the brightest full moon they had seen; appearing so large as to cause a sort of confusion. They studied it and looked at each other and studied it some more: the reflected light held them. As it had every man who has ever lived. An unending synchronous rotation with Earth and a never-failing reflection of the sun's light. On this night it appeared as the heart of a mythology or legend and it served to trivialize by way of mathematics and geology any workings of mankind; any rise or fall in the world of men.

Trout continued to surface. Each dimple in the water caught the moonlight then faded to a flat calm. Fish moon, the man said as he picked up his paddle. I think that's the fish moon. The paddle cut the water and they pushed forward. Their eyes moved between the riseforms and the pale pink moon. The boy looked back at the man who did not say anything further. He laid the rod across the thwarts and began to paddle in rhythm with the man.

Kemuel DeMoville

Plumeria Stars

Characters

Brother: A Young Man bound by guilt.

Sister: A Young Woman bound by fear. She's a soldier. She has a history with the Bound Man.

Bound Man: A Man, unable to move his body, he struggles for every breath. He is in a wheelchair or something resembling a wheelchair. Brother cares for him.

Lover: A Woman bound by love.

Setting

A dining room. What little furniture is there is rusted, dusty, and only partially functional.

(Brother, Sister, Lover, and Bound Man have all gathered for a meal. Sister, the soldier, is on leave. Lover is meeting Sister's family for the first time. They sit around a dinner table.)

Brother

So this is. It's really great. Having you home.

Sister

Yeah.

Bound Man

So great.

Brother

Yeah. This is nice. Does anyone want more chicken?

Lover

No. I'm stuffed.

Brother

It's KFC.

Lover

Well. It seemed like homemade.

Bound Man

You want to hear a joke?

Lover

Sure.

Bound Man

Why did the elephant drink so much?

Lover

I don't know. Why?

Bound Man

To forget.

Sister

Hilarious.

(In unison, everyone, including the Bound Man, pounds the table hard—Boom! All freeze except Sister.)

Sister

Pull over. Let me drive. You've been drinking. I know you've been drinking. Don't touch the wheel.

(They pound the table again: Boom! They unfreeze.)

Bound Man

Well. They can't all be funny.

Sister

Yeah. God forbid a joke is funny.

Bound Man

So you tell one.

Sister

I don't remember anything funny.

(Silence)

Brother

So. How are things over there?

Sister

Shit.

Brother

You scc anything? Any action?

Sister

I don't want to talk about it.

Brother

Save any lives?

(Again: Boom! All freeze but Brother.)

Brother

Don't touch her! You fucking asshole! Pull over! Pull over! You fucking …

(Boom! They unfreeze.)

Sister

I don't want to talk about it.

Brother

Yeah. Okay, sorry.

Bound Man

Some other time.

Sister

No.

Lover

So your sister tells me that you just graduated High School last year. What have you been up to?

Brother

Nothing.

Bound Man

Wiping my ass.

Lover

Oh.

Brother

Not just that.

Bound Man

There's also the internet porn.

Sister

I'm not here to watch my brother get hassled by Darth Vader. Lay off.

Bound Man

Don't tell me what to do.

(Boom! All freeze but the Bound Man.)

Bound Man

I'm fine. Quit trying to pick everything I do apart. One drink. One fuckin' drink. Shut up and look out your window.

(Boom! All unfreeze.)

Lover

I'm not trying to be rude, but I don't know who you are.

Bound Man

I was thinking the same thing about you.

                    Brother

He's. He's family.

                     Sister

No, he's not.

                   Bound Man

I'm the father of her child.

                     Lover

Oh. Oh. I … I didn't know.

                     Sister

Asshole.

                     Lover

Where … Where is?

                   Bound Man

He's dead. He died.

                     Lover

Oh. Oh God. You should have told me. I…

                     Sister

Don't. Don't. Don't.

  (Boom! They're all in the car, the Lover crying softly like a baby. They speak over one
                            another.)

                     Sister

Pull over. Let me drive.

                   Bound Man

I'm fine. Quit trying to pick everything I do apart.

                     Sister

You've been drinking.

                   Bound Man

One fuckin' drink.

                     Sister

I know you've been drinking.

                   Bound Man

Shut up and look out your window.

                    Brother

Don't touch her! You fucking asshole! Pull over!

Sister

Don't touch the wheel!

Brother

Pull over! You fucking …

(Boom! They crash. Stillness for a moment. Then the Sister lets out a guttural moan that becomes a scream—as if something is being torn out of her body—then silence.)

Bound Man

When I was a child, I would look up at the night sky. Look up at the stars. I thought they were Plumeria blossoms. Hanging on some far-off branch. Like when you lie at the beach. In the shade of a Plumeria tree. And you see the blossoms hanging overhead. I had forgotten that. That image. The Plumeria star. The way children connect things that have no meaning. No relationship. Not really, but it seems like they should. I had forgotten about that. Until I was lying on the beach with my son. In the shade of a Plumeria tree. And looking up to the sky he smiled, "Look, Daddy. Stars." Fuck. Fuck.

Tom Driscoll
Ingratitude

am grateful to be alive in 2020, grateful to bear witness to the Age of Covid in the Trump Era, grateful for the response to the pandemic playing out here in the U.S. by a new generation of frontline health care providers, first responders, local government officials, scientists, parents, students. In addition, I am grateful for streaming services and bingeing, late-night talk show hosts, Notorious RGB, Dr. Anthony Fauci, the local IGA grocery and its many essential employees, and Zoom and Zooming. And dreaming.

Gratitude. And dreams. Dreams define who we are. Whether wandering the abstract cartoonland of sleep-lit neural highways and back alleys, or trekking the endless paths of pure aspiration, dreams guide individuals, communities, nations, and cultures into the future. Whereas 2020 has been a good year for curling up in bed and working out lockdown life in the abstract, it's not been such a good year for dreaming big dreams.

Grateful as I am for the next generations, I can't escape the dissonant reactions I feel for them in the Age of Covid. On one hand, millions of high school and college students, in-coming freshmen and outgoing seniors have largely been denied their institutional rites of passage thanks to Covid. On the other hand, 2020 is and will forever be a date to reckon with, the year when the collective power of dreams stood toe to toe with death and protest and destruction.

I remember my protracted coming of age in the late 60s and well into the mid-70s, leaving high school, starting college as a cub editor and reporter. Gradually radicalized covering events of 1968, I soon found myself without a scholarship and drafted. When I returned home, my views on the treatment of Black men were informed by racism in the Army. Then a sudden marriage and a child, and more college. My head exploded with fully formed responsibilities and raw creative energy. Mine was a dream-filled coming-of-age disrupted by my staunch opposition to the Vietnam War, support for the civil rights struggle, pursuit of elusive muses, and the uncontrollable compulsion to write about it all.

That tumultuous first decade as an adult ended about the time Ronald Reagan became president. I arranged my principles into a mental toolbox and embarked on becoming an American in the sense that I poked my head up from the underground into the realities of mainstream citizenry. Revolution by masquerade I called it.

I pulled the grocery bag off my head: cut my hair and shaved my beard. Then I left America to spend much of the next decade working in Africa, beginning with 2 ½ years in Peace Corps. My wife and I eventually ended up inside the Beltway, Northern Virginia, three blocks from the East Falls Church Metro station and the Orange Line.

In a dreamlike reversal of a rebellious youth, gratitude slowly replaced bitterness toward my native land. With profound reservations, I allowed myself to feel pride again about being an American, regardless of who lived in the White House. But so enchanted was I with all my highfalutin adult perspicacity, boyish patriotism and business class upgrades, I didn't notice that somewhere on the road to the Twenty-first Century, all the principled tools in my toolbox had timed out; they had become obsolete.

History is not going to separate the pandemic of 2020 from the reign of Donald Trump. Coronavirus-2019 in the Trump Era is a tragic farce. Covid has become emotional shorthand for death in quarantine lying flat on your belly tethered to a breathing tube.

It is also cultural code now for the creeping rift between compassion and liberty; old and young; masks and militias; compromised immunity and raging hormones; social distancing and religious observance; commuting by bicycle and mob-spread by chopper; community transmission and community; weddings, reunions and funerals, and funerals.

Nor will history forget the summer of 2020, how the murder of George Floyd brought quarantine numb protestors into the streets of Minneapolis. Many wore masks. Many did not. Covid had suddenly become an afterthought. When protestors marched from 38th and Chicago over to the MPD Third Precinct headquarters, what happened next would brand the social justice demonstrations with violent disregard for life and property.

Looters and arsonists hijacked the right of the people to peaceably assemble and petition the government for a redress of grievance. The scene at the Third Precinct, abandoned by police and set on fire while rioters destroyed the adjacent commercial district, would serve as a template of injustice and rage for cities across the U.S. and around the world.

I popped open my toolbox to grasp righteous indignation and found every one of my principled gadgets from the past had corroded due to lack of use and caked completely white with the privilege of not being a Black man.

The matter of Black lives, the importance of equality and justice, principles that I had once wielded defiantly, needed a serious upgrade. I cannot ignore the fact that the longer my principles had languished in white privilege, the more irrelevant they became to the day-to-day concerns of Black, Brown, Indigenous and LGBTQ people.

For so many opportunities and second chances to dream, too many to list or even remember them all, I am grateful. But 2020 has reminded me that as with any colonial or post-colonial, race- and class-biased system, societal opportunities often come at the expense of someone being denied them. It's going to take a while for privileged white society to adapt to the entirely new reality that 2020 has brought into focus. 2020 will never go away.

It is the demonstrated ingratitude for fragile white America's unsolicited gift to non-whites of inequality that I am perhaps most grateful for in the fall of 2020. Most ungrateful, I am, in my heart, for allowing myself to slip slowly into white privilege and white primacy—like the storied frog in a pot, unaware till the water is about to boil over into the streets that it is too late to change the outcome.

The 400-year struggle for social justice continues. Certainly, in the media, arts and entertainment world, the struggle continues for representation, opportunities and second chances in a milieu dominated by white and white male privilege. Covid-19 will remain a threat so long as Americans remain divided politically. That means people of color will continue to be at greater risk of contracting and dying from the virus.

Redress for this is complicated by the infrastructure of white privilege in every socioeconomic sector of American life. As Dr. King famously said, "The arc of the moral universe is long, but it bends toward justice." It is not just magical thinking to believe this is a human truism. Nor is it realistic to think that humans do not have to, from time to time, mount the arc of the moral universe in prodigious numbers in order to speed up bending the arc closer and closer to the ideal of justice for all.

The Age of Covid in the Trump Era gives us much to be grateful for, including ingratitude for the murder of Black men and women under the knee of police, including the disproportionate number of Blacks, Browns and other minorities, and senior citizens in nursing homes, dying from the novel virus. 2020 has exposed fault lines, terrible societal weaknesses, systemic institutional racism, and a failure of whites to ally with people of color, first peoples, immigrants, and the poor.

I'm sick and tired of Trump Era political rhetoric. This lying grifter in the White House, and his gang of enablers, and the gaggle of his base has got to go. So please vote. Then be prepared to demonstrate the courage of your convictions and do what you know is right, continue to fight for social justice and equality, and continue to dream.

2020 Poetry Collections Sampler

Folk Opera Extra

A Taste of 3 New Poetry Collections from
Up On Big Rock Poetry Series
a Shipwreckt Books Imprint

SHIPWRECKT BOOKS PUBLISHING COMPANY

New from Up On Big Rock Poetry Series

Summer 2020

www.shipwrecktbooks.press

Delta Eddy

Four Sparks

From *Sparks* (Up On Big Rock Poetry Series, 2020)

The Origin of Libraries
for the dedication of the "library of the future"
I find myself walking through deep snow
in the wrong shoes. Every step breaks the
    rimey crust
and I plunge ahead, wet and cold to my knees
    until
I come onto the deer trail.

Every ungulate print has something in it—
bark shred, dry leaf, deer scat— like a row
of open books I look into and follow up
through the woods, around treefall and
    brambles.
The red halo in the snow under the scat means
 there are still dried berries up on the ridge.
The pawed-up spots are where moss used to
    be.
How on this cold earth to live? Read,
my teachers told me, read everything.
                    *
In The Great Library of Alexandria, Egypt, we
collected all the alphabets of Babel, the news
from Khartoum, and the sky maps of Ptolemy.
Then Romans came and burned whole
    languages up,
so sand would wash those kingdoms away. Not
    one
brick nor book beside another. We stood in the
    smoke,
gathered what we could save and started over.

The human trail broke up into pathless prints
 among the brambles, where we have lived
    since,
hemmed round by Huns and Vandals,
    rewriting
our lost books, turning skirmishes into myths
    and myths
into wars, turning wars into words and words

into love of words.
                    *
The origins of this library are in trees and sand.
The lost language of trees is written into books;
sand that binds these bricks holds flakes of
    mica
lit like stars.

Following the writing in the snow, the deer
sense a seam through bare trees: the owl's trail
up the ridge to the open sky.

The Mother of Gods
As it happened, the sky
was tired of holding himself up and fell
asleep on the earth, who was herself
exhausted from inventing the birds
and making herself green all the time.

They slept a long time.
Earth dreamed of insects in
a million shapes. The sky dreamed,
like every one of us,
of new ways of fucking the earth.

As it also happened, the sky's wet dream
made a big mess all over the earth. But they
slept on, the sky smiling. So
that is what made the first being, Agdistis,
both a goddess and a god.

Agdistis grew up on the sleeping earth
like any redwood or butterfly or mountain
in a world that was only green and blue,
mother and father, songs and storms.
Stopped to pick a daffodil. "Ai ai," they sighed.

With that pluck, earth awoke and saw this
    creature.

so much like her and so much like the sky, with
    a womb
like hers, full of gods, and the balls and phallus
    of the father
who now thundered awake and aroused.
    Agdistis trembled.
The colors of that dawn still glow every
    morning, somewhere.

The sky poured down on Adgistis, as he poured
    himself on earth,
and found what earth already knew. Is this one
    to be ravished or
a rival to kill? Daughter and son. The one that
    is two.
The sky turned dark. Night fell across earth
    who made
a white drop of mercy pass across the face of
    the sky.

Agdistis was many at once, as much daffodil
as man, as much man as woman, as much
    woman as
a sunrise. The father struck off the phallus
and stuck it in the ground. Immediately it
    sprouted
leaves and bore almonds. The balls rolled away.

She was she alone, no longer of the mother,
the shadow of the sky falling on a body no
    longer hers,
alone on a world that needed names and
    creatures
to clean up the bloody mess. That is how we
    came to love
Kybele, the mother of gods who lives beyond
    the sky.

Why I Love Slimy Texas Blues

I mean guitar licks pointy enough
to kill the roaches in the corners while
the percussion boosts your shoulders like the
    thud
of a dead dog under a fast car. The singer
takes side bets on Otis Redding being alive

and fronting a band in Brownsville.
All the women in the place are thinking, *I've been
loving you too long.* All the men think,
I can't stop now. Every man betrayed, all the
    women
left in the lurch, each ecstatic to be sole
proprietor of such grief, remembering the slow
dance in the kitchen with bodies to saxophones
swaying like buildings before they fall down.

Poetry

I have been wondering since you asked,
what has become of our hunger
for poetry? We no longer
linger in bookstores yearning
for manna from pages, the sky
that opened once is dry
now. Are all our gods dead
or silent or repeating themselves?
I alphabetize my shelves
in case I need a poem to illustrate
a point or to fill a lecture or a minute
before sleep. There's less of love in it
and more of judgment.

Or is poetry a long marriage: years of passion
then years of tender, if silent, concern?
Where will I ever learn
so much of love and give back
just my spindly mind
and time? I miss the wine
the candles and my new wife's nakedness.
Every kiss, every poem a new soul.

Or else I grow into the old husk
Yeats warned me about and
Dylan Thomas sang to sleep.
My words are dutiful, my attention
too cheap. Old friend,
ever since you asked,
I miss myself but just now see
a book on my shelf I have to read.

Steve McCown
The Ghost of Four
From *Ghosting* (Up On Big Rock Poetry Series, 2020)

Dirty Laundry
Even then I relished sound,
dropping tennis shoes down a laundry chute.
A whoosh, a thud rose up to me,
and an enlivening backlash
of tunneled wind.

I tipped a dictionary into the abyss.
The weight of words
banged and echoed against the tin shaft,
the definitions resonating
in the vertical chamber,
a belly-flat climatic plunk at the bottom.

I dropped my voices as well:
a whisper, a yell, a scream.
High in my parents' home, I spoke
through three floors into the basement,
to the basement—an underworld
I feared, placated with speech,
frightened with sheer noise.

Unaware I was listening
(I was unaware it could speak)
the subterranean spoke once:
Claire, our laundry woman, alone,
hot iron in hand, ranting to herself,
sweating and swearing over my shirts,
my sheets, my towels, my pants.

Men's Room
At a Greyhound Bus Depot
two poets stand side by side at the urinals,
rigid as fence posts.
Between them is a partial divider.

Rusty chrome fixtures blur and distort
their reflected faces.

Each knows the other's picture and poems,
but they have never met until now—
only now they haven't anything to say
to each other out of embarrassment,
and eyes up, nothing to see except a white-tiled wall
scribbled with graffiti: "Bill stood here."
"For a good time call 645-3211."

The Uses of the Dead
Tracked on, the bear
carpeted our cabin,
spread-eagled on the floor
as if fallen from a great height
and anchored,
a coffee table centered on his back.

Chairs were arranged
around his frayed edges,
where adults talked
about fishing and hunting
over his skull, glass eyes fixed
on a blackened hearth.

I played with the bear,
my fingers stepping gingerly
into a gaping mouth:
an intrepid explorer shadowed
by rows of stalagmites and stalactites.

At night he was my bed,
a sleeping bag unfurled

as if in the heart of a wild black forest.

There, knowing the uses of the dead,
I could fly, riding his skin.

Ghosting the Pages

History in my hand:
a small blue address book decades old,
phone numbers included,
found in a forgotten drawer in my desk.

Here's a number
I could not live without
until it became unlisted,
and here's one
I circled with red ink
again and again.
It isn't working now.

Here's a former friend,
his number's crossed out
for reasons crossed out in my head.
Another pal changed his name
and now he's off the record.

Always moving then,
an old lover has a series
of addresses, a timeline, a map,
leading to blank pages
at the end of my book.

I turn back.
Like a jealous lover,
I trace the imprint of a number,
ink faded,
the impressions rising slowly,
ghosting the page.

Louis Martinelli

Four for Van Gogh

From *Dreaming with Open Eyes, Poems for Vincent Van Gogh* (Up On Big Rock Poetry Series, 2020)

Van Gogh's Ear
Scorned for visiting brothels
Having sold only one painting
In his lifetime
Failure growing
Inside him like a tumor
Van Gogh decides
To cut off his ear
Which he gives to Rachel
A prostitute
At the House Of Tolerance
Telling her "Keep this
And treasure it." And
When she later puts it
To her ear – a sea shell
Covered with blood -
She hears the wind blowing
Through olive trees
The scraping of a knife
In a kitchen
And three grows
Flying across the luminous sky
Of Provence.

Beauty
We make love
In the dark
Because the body
Will turn blue one day
Be pumped dry
Filled with chemicals
Or burned to ash
Gravity will take
Its most seductive
Features
And hang them

Like gourds
Like twisted vines
Even the burls of trees
Will be more comely
Than the furrowed skin
That was once
Smooth as satin.
In the dark womb
Of his mother
Van Gogh
Was already dreaming
With open eyes
And in the light
Thirty-six years later
He would lie down
In an olive grove
Because he said
Like the body of a woman
It was too beautiful
To imagine or paint.

Van Gogh Writes to Shakespeare's Wife
For Germaine Greer
I feel toward you a tenderness
I've never felt
Toward any other woman.
Eight years your husband's senior
A country girl
Who herded cows, fed your lamb,
Practiced the arts of cooking and knitting,
Understood the courtship sonnets
William wrote to gain your favor -
It puzzles me
How you've disappeared
Like a photograph in a fire
Even your ashes reviled.

But then, you're in such company:
Those wives of great men of letters
Who nursed children
In empty marriage beds
As husbands prowled the world
In search of love, fame, inspiration.
I think we could have been happy, Anne:
After all, I didn't get along with men
Or make an art that causes kings to swoon.
My crimes were failure and insanity,
Yours being born female and too soon.

I Dream Van Gogh's Ear Is Orbiting The Earth

Illegally –
The snail of the inner ear
The cochlea
Sending out waves
Of B-flat harmony
The tympanic membrane
Of the drum
Played by a circle
Of men
Who don't frighten
Children
Will not make war
On anyone.

About the Contributors

Emilio DeGrazia, MY VIRAL SUMMER VACATION: Emilio published several books, including two with Shipwreckt Books Press—a collection of essays called *Eye Shadow*, and *Shamu, Splash and Solemna*, a book featuring Carol Stoa Senn's creative work. He and his wife Monica also have co-edited anthologies of Minnesota writing, and he has served two terms as Winona's Poet Laureate. His second book of poetry is *What Trees Know* (Nodin, 2020).

Larry Gavin, AN ASSEMBLAGE OF TROUBLES: MAY 26, 2020: Larry is the author of five books of poetry. He worked for fifteen years as a senior editor at *Midwest Fly Fishing Magazine*. Currently, he writes about outdoor and environmental issues on a freelance basis. He lives in Faribault, Minnesota, where he wanders the woods and fields with his wife Patty, and a beagle named Doc.

Julie A. Ryan, THE THOUGHTS OF A POLAR BEAR: **Julie** is a novelist, essayist, poet, and visual artist. Her timely *When Life Was Still* trilogy was released on the eve of the pandemic. Julie's essays have been published in Minnesota newspapers and various blogs. *The Clothesline Review* has contained her fiction. And her poetry has appeared in a variety of publications, including *Writers' Night - A Sense of Place*, 2017; Northfield Sidewalk Poetry, 2018; and the End in Mind Pandemic Poetry Project, 2020.

Louis Martinelli, THE DAY THE VIRUS CAME: Louis Martinelli, poet, playwright, essayist and educator, is a graduate of St. Mary's University and The University of Cincinnati. He has been a Writer in Residence in many Midwestern communities and organizations, including The Mayo Clinic and The Northfield Arts Guild. His play *Wild Iris* has been performed in theatres, medical centers, and conferences in the United States and Europe. Another of his plays, *Take My Hand*, won a National Endowment for The Arts outstanding achievement award. In 2001, Martinelli was nominated for a MacArthur Foundation Award for his work in helping create sustainable communities. Literary executor of environmental writer Paul Gruchow's estate as well as founder and director of The Paul Gruchow Foundation, Louis is most recently author of the collection *Dreaming with Open Eyes*, *Poems for Vincent Van Gogh* (Up On Big Rock Poetry Series, 2020).

Emilio Regina, MY UNCLE AND THE CORONA: Emilio is a retired high school Drama/English teacher. He presently works as an English auxiliary instructor at The College of the Rockies. He is a multi-instrumentalist and is a front man for the blues band The Hollers. Emilio is also a published playwright with several publishers across Canada and the U.S. Emilio lives in Kimberley, British Columbia, Vancouver.

Jennifer Wang, जल्द ही: Jennifer's fiction comes out of the struggles of her Indian-Chinese family members to survive the slums of Mumbai. After pursuing several careers, graduating from Harvard Law School, and raising a family, in 2018 she founded the Stanford Alumni Fiction Writers' group, dedicated to the critique and support of local writers. Recently, her short story DEMON KING was published by *Green Hills Literary Lantern* and THE BLESSING was published by *After The Happy Hour Review*.

Becky Boling, CABIN 9: Becky is retired from Carleton College, where she taught and published on contemporary Latin American literature, Becky began publishing her creative work with a short story, CASSANDRA EN SU TORRE DE PAPEL, at Proyecto Sherezade. Her poetry has appeared in journals and magazines such as *Willows Wept Review, Martin Lake Journal, Persimmon Tree*. She has won contests, the Northfield Sidewalk Poetry competition and the Red Wing Arts' 19th Poet-Artist Collaboration. She even contributed lines to a crowdsourced, community poem created by Kwame Alexander on NPR in 2020. Becky lives and writes in Northfield, Minnesota.

Steve McCown, Two Pandemic Poems: Steve is a recently retired high school and parttime college teacher. He graduated with a B.A. in English from Winona State University and with an M.A. in English from Northern Arizona University. After teaching in the deserts of southern California and Arizona for over 30 years, Steve returned to his native Minnesota, to Northfield, where he now resides with his wife Barbara and two semi-content cats. His debut collection of poetry, *Ghosting*, (Up On Big Rock Poetry Series, 2020) has just been released.

Jim Johnson, Hooks: Jim Emeritus Poet Laureate of Duluth, is the author of the collection *Text for Our Nomadic Future* (Red Dragonfly Press, 20180). He has been writing his fishing memoirs. He lives in Cedar Falls, Iowa, in the spring and summer so he can fish the Driftless Area. Then he summers in Isabella, Minnesota.

Waliyullah Tunde Abimbola, The Suicide Episode: Waliyullah is an undergraduate student of English at Obafemi Awolowo University, Ile-Ife. He enjoys reading and writing all genres of literature a lot, and lives in Ile-Ife, a town in Southwest Nigeria.

A. S. Arcilesi, Plastic Breath: Alfredo Salvatore Arcilesi has spent a decade penning award-winning short- and feature-length screenplays, while working as a full-time artisan baker. His prose work explores the trials and tribulations of ordinary people embedded in ordinary and extraordinary environments and conflicts. Alfredo's short stories have appeared in over 45 literary journals worldwide, and he was a finalist in the Blood Orange Review Literary Contest. In addition to several short pieces, he is currently working on his debut novel.

James Petrillo, Twice Feckless: James hails from beautiful Lanesboro, Minnesota, where he lives with his family. After his university studies, he worked in theatre, both children's and professional, before becoming a television producer. Upon returning to his hometown, he independently released a novel, *The Darkwood*, a horror thriller. His true heart lives in the fantasy realm of magic, swords, and dragons, and he has written fantasy most of his life He is the author most recently of the fantasy epic *Ashyer* (Rocket Science Press, 2018).

Michael Crane, Corona Road: Michael is a consulting environmental economist, carpenter, father of two and grandfather of three. He carries an overweighted backpack full of stories from his travels. This is his first attempt to get one down on paper. He lives where he works and sometimes at his home in Vermont.

Janet Preus, My House Is on Fire, But I'm Not in It: Janet is a writer, editor and playwright. She directed a college theater program before becoming a radio news reporter, the news editor of a daily newspaper, and eventually a magazine editor. Published pieces include personal essays, a musical, a series of children's books, theater reviews and numerous trade magazine articles.

Dan Butterfass, Sweat Lodge: Dan is a part-time resident of rural Filmore County, Minnesota, where he lives in a remote cabin from which he parses his time with his Labrador retriever and other friends as a dedicated fly-fishing trout angler, avid upland bird hunter, meat-seeking deer hunter, novice beekeeper, backroads wanderer, amateur botanist, snowshoeing enthusiast, birdwatcher, and woodchopper, while also pursuing the lost art of walking the countryside with no particular destination in mind.

Neale Torgrimson, THEY ARE COMING UP YOUR STREET: Neale's last story for this magazine, DEPARTMENT OF CATASTROPHES, appeared in the Winter 2018 issue. A graduate of the University of Minnesota, he lives and works in Minneapolis.

Wm. Anthony Connolly, SAINT ALBINO THOMAS: A MURDER: William is the author of three novels: *The Jenny Muck, Get Back* and *The Obituaries*, which was a Canadian bestseller in 2005. His work has appeared in *The Rumpus, Intellectual Refuge* and *Elephant Journal* to name a few. He is on the faculty of the MFA in Writing at Lindenwood University, and a contributing editor with *Talking Writing*. He earned a Ph.D. in English and Creative Writing from the University of Missouri and also holds an MFA in Writing from Goddard College. He lives in the Midwest with his wife Dyan and their two dogs, Hemingway Short Story and Professor Leo Tolstoy. His latest novel is *The Naked Sea* will be released by Kellogg Press in 2021.

Lee Henschel Jr., R: Lee began his writing life when he was twelve and has never put down his pen. His short stories, poems and essays have appeared in numerous anthologies, and his epic historical fiction series, *The Sailing Master* (Rocket Science Press, 2013, 2017 & 2019) has been nominated for a Minnesota Book Award, and a Midwest Independent Publishers Association award. He lives in Minneapolis, Minnesota.

Rob Hardy, TWO VARIATIONS: Rob is the first Poet Laureate of Northfield, Minnesota, and the author of *Domestication: Collected Poems 1996-2016* (Up On Big Rock Poetry Series, 2017).

Raymond Luczak, THE CROW LADY: Raymond is the author and editor of 24 books, including *Compassion, Michigan: The Ironwood Stories* (Modern History Press) and *once upon a twin: poems* (Gallaudet University Press, forthcoming in February 2021). His work has appeared in *Poetry, Bellingham Review, Passages North*, and elsewhere. A ten-time Pushcart Prize nominee and an inaugural Zoeglossia Fellow, he lives in Minneapolis, Minnesota.

David Patt, COVID TIME: David is a writer, editor and scholar. Prior to pandemic travel restrictions he divided his time between Manila and his home in Cambridge, MA.

Mercury-Marvin Sunderland, TWO POEMS: Mercury-Marvin (he/him) is a Hellenist transgender autistic gay man from Seattle with Borderline Personality Disorder. He currently attends the Evergreen State College and works for *Headline Poetry & Press*. Since 2019, his work has appeared in numerous journals such as Antioch University *LA's Lunch Ticket Magazine*, UC Santa Barbara's Spectrum Literary Journal, UC Riverside's Santa Ana River Review, University of Texas at San Antonio's *Sagebrush Review*, University of Wisconsin-Parkside's *Straylight Magazine*, University of Wyoming's *Owen Wister Review*, and The New School's *The Inquisitive Eater*.

Roger McKnight, VICTORIA: Roger hails from the southern Illinois city of Little Egypt. He now lives in Minnesota. After college at SIUC, he lived and worked in Chicago, Sweden, and Puerto Rico. In Sweden he saw the value of gender equity. In Puerto Rico he witnessed the dignity of life on the island before the U.S. government abandoned it in post-hurricane days. Roger has taught Scandinavian Studies in Minnesota. He's published short fiction in literary journals. His latest book *Hopeful Monsters* (London UK: Storgy Books, 2019) features short stories from Minnesota, Scandinavia, and the Midwest.

Imani Skipwith THE PALM OF DEATH'S Hand: Imani is an eighteen-year-old college freshman attending Belhaven University. She is currently majoring in creative writing to pursue a career in publishing. She recently won a national gold medal for her short story VOI TOÏ and a silver medal for her poetry collection *The Nelson-Dortch Cemetery* in the 2020 Scholastics Art and Writing Awards.

D.E. Green, FOUR POEMS, D. E. (Doug) Green teaches literature, creative writing, composition, and gender and queer studies at Augsburg University. He has published many articles on Shakespeare, regular reviews of productions for *Shakespeare Bulletin*, general-interest essays, and poetry. His poem GRATITUDE won the 2018 Martin Lake Journal Bookend Prize. His poems also appear on the sidewalks of Northfield, MN. Doug likes to say that he has been an occasional poet for over 35 years. *Jumping the Median*, (Encircle Publications, 2019) was D.E.'s debut collection.

Justin Watkins, FISH MOON: Justin was born in the top right corner of Minnesota and now lives with his wife and two sons in the bottom right corner of the state. He walks trout streams, wades carp flats and paddles with family and friends. He graduated from St. Olaf College in 1998. His chapbook, *Bottom Right Corner*, won the 2014 Red Dragonfly Press Emergence Chapbook Competition. He is the author of *A Mark of Permanence* (Up On Big Rock Press, 2018).

Kemuel DeMoville, PLUMERIA STARS: Kemuel is an award-winning poet and playwright whose work has been produced internationally every year since 2005. He has an MFA in playwriting from the University of Hawaii at Manoa, and an MA in syncretic theatre from Victoria University of Wellington in Aotearoa, New Zealand. His work has been published by *Spider Magazine*, *YouthPLAYS, Heuer Publishing, Sediments Literary-Arts Journal, Meow Meow Pow Pow*, and is included in *222 MORE Comedy Monologue*s, an anthology from Smith and Kraus Publishers.

Tom Driscoll, INGRATITUDE: Tom is Managing editor and CEO of Shipwreckt Books and *Lost Lake Folk Opera* magazine. He is the author of *Ondine & the Blue Troll, Selected Short Works* (Rocket Science Press, 2013).

Delta Eddy, FOUR SPARKS: Delta (*nee* Gary) Eddy is Professor of English at Winona State University where she has taught for over 30 years. She holds a doctorate from Binghamton University and an MFA from the University of Arizona. She has played American roots music in bars and coffeehouses since the 1970s in ensembles and solo. She has given readings around the U.S. She is married to the artist Marykay Lind Eddy and they live on a butterfly ranch in Dodge County, Minnesota. Delta, a poet, is author of *Sparks* (Up On Big Rock Poetry Series, 2020).

Covid-19 2020